HOMETOWN FOLKS

Hometown Folks

A FINNISH-AMERICAN SAGA

Gerald F. Carlson

NORTH STAR PRESS OF ST. CLOUD, INC.

To Carly
who may someday want to know.

Acknowledgments

Not many books are written without some outside help. This one is no exception. I'm indebted to a number of people whose names I either never knew or can't remember—the lady at the Missoula (Montana) Public Library who searched out the old newspaper articles detailing the shooting in that city, the staffs at the Minnesota State Hospital in St. Peter, Minnesota, and the Veterans Administration regional offices at Fort Snelling, Minnesota, who helped piece together the tragedy of my uncle Nick. Special thanks go to my aunt Alena Carlson-Becklund-Marsyla, whose assistance is detailed in the foreword. Finally, a singular kudos to Miss Marianne Jones, my instructor at a two-week Elderhostel memoir-writing course at the University of Iowa. She read the manuscript in its rough form and came up with numerous solid, valid, valuable suggestions. I didn't follow all of them. No reason . . . except, maybe, a male ego thing.

G.F.C.

Special editorial assistance by Amy J. Kopperude.

Copyright © 1997 Gerald F. Carlson

ISBN: 0-87839-115-0

Printed in the United States of America by Versa Press, Inc., East Peoria, Illinois.

Published by: North Star Press of St. Cloud, Inc.
P.O. Box 451
St. Cloud, Minnesota 56302

Foreword

_____

This book did not start out to be one. It simply evolved from an idle curiosity about my forebears' lives and times.

Throughout my adolescence, usually in an effort to impress upon me that I never had it so good, my father sometimes talked about his boyhood: what it was like growing up in a family of fourteen children, the meager existence they endured, and how they managed to survive among the swamps and bogs of the glacier-scoured land of northern Minnesota. I didn't pay a lot of attention; it is an axiom of history that, as one moves backward in time, the snow is always deeper, the temperatures colder, and the miles longer.

The years slipped by taking their expected toll. Then the day came when my father was gone. I looked around and suddenly realized that most of the fourteen were also in their graves. A rare moment of Americana was about to be lost. Determined that at least some of their story be recorded, I began jotting down everything about them I could remember, things I had heard and events in which I had participated or witnessed. The effort produced enough material to make me want to go on. I started digging into court records, old newspapers, military and Veterans Administration files. They all added a little, each piece building on the whole and often nudging still another forgotten item from the hidden files of the subconscious.

When word got out that I was nosing around, I began to hear from relatives I didn't know I had. Their concern, although they didn't say so, was that I might write something that would be an embarrassment for them or, even worse, that I might make a dollar. It was obvious that they were not going to be much help. Then, I found a truly interested source of information—my father's youngest sister, Alena Marsyla. Aunt Alena, a spightly lady in her eighties, was an is a fountain of knowledge about her family. Her memory is superb. Not that she was always willing to reveal some of the things she knew about her siblings. Usually, however, if I coaxed and was patient, she would eventually decide to divulge some bits and particles of bone from the group's closeted skeletons, prefaced with, "Well, maybe you can write it so it won't sound so bad."

Finally, I could see a book and have tried to "write it so it won't sound so bad" without sacrificing the integrity of the story.

I have no doubt some will feel that it would have been better to let the past die. I cannot agree. History is inviolate and must never be compromised. As far as I am concerned, my generation's progenitors were all, each and every one of them, jewels in their own way. Some of the diamonds may have been a bit rough around the edges, but they were diamonds all the same.

The community I called home up to the age of sixteen and the focus of events for the majority of the characters in the story, Cloquet, Minnesota, is nearly always mispronounced by outsiders. The natives say Klo-Kay. They live there, so they should know. Neither the town's historical society nor the public library are much help as to the origin of the name, but a good guess is that it came from a very early sawmill operator who disappeared into the bark dust and timber slashings of bygone times.

A few years ago in the West Coast city where I reside today, I chanced to see in the newspaper that a new priest, a Father Cloquet, had been assigned to one of the local parishes. I called him. He'd never heard of Cloquet, Minnesota, but he agreed that the name is pronouced Klo-Kay.

I have, in some instances, changed the names of non-family characters for reasons that will be obvious to the reader, but all, regardless of name, are or were real people.

Contents

The Carlson Family

The Parents

Nikolai Karlsson*: born December 6, 1859
died November 20, 1937
Marjana Mattila-Karlson: born June 10, 1867**
died September 20, 1932

The Children (in order of birth)

Ida: born September 7, 1889
died March 10, 1971

Hilda: born September 23, 1890
died April 27, 1965

Olga: born November 20, 1891
died June 13, 1968

Lucy: born May 12, 1893
died December 30, 1966

Alex: born August 3, 1894
died May 16, 1934

Nick: born December 28, 1896
died October 4, 1957

Swen: born August 1, 1898
died December 21, 1970

Frank: born March 20, 1900
died February 17, 1977

John: born May 31, 1901
died August 2, 1945

Charley: born April 18, 1903
died November 14, 1957

Alena: born July 9, 1905
died —

Willie: born December 6, 1906
died June 18, 1980

Oscar: born April 11, 1908
died October 1, 1973

Jalmer: born November 29, 1909
died July 3, 1991

* Name changed to Karlson after he arrived in the United States. All his children spelled the name Carlson.
** Various documents have different month and day birth dates; others are: September 7, 1867, and October 5, 1867.

1

Beginnings

I was born on December 25, 1925—Christmas Day for most, labor day for my mother. The blessed event, not likely to have been particularly noted by the community, took place in the small town of Iron Mountain, Michigan, where Henry Ford was recruiting workers for his Model T body plant and offering an unheard-of five dollars a day to get them. My father, Frank Edward Carlson, twenty-five years old and unable to resist the lure of big wages, heeded Ford's call. Bundling his pregnant wife, Alice Margaret Jorgensen-Carlson, and a large short-haired hound named Buddy into his 1923 Model T touring car, he headed eastward, isinglass side curtains flapping like the wings on a startled partridge, to the Wolverine State and aced me out of a Minnesota genesis.

We lived in upper Michigan for about a year after I was born, but I don't remember any of it. Ford soon went to all-metal bodies, negating his need for Upper Peninsula timber, and closed his Iron Mountain operation. My folks, their new family member in tow, backtracked "home" to Cloquet, Minnesota. Buddy didn't make the return trip. Obsessively devoted to my mother, he wouldn't allow anyone he didn't know to get remotely near her. Somebody apparently took offense. Buddy was poisoned by a person or persons unknown. Twenty-eight years later, I went miles out of my way to drive through the town of my birth. I wasn't any more impressed with it than it had been with me.

My earliest childhood recollection is of urinating. I must have been about three years old. I was standing, peeing into a chamber pot and making fun of my brother Richard, who, attempting to be a big boy like me, wet his pants because he was too young to manage the buttons on his rompers. My mother, of course, scolded me for teas-

1

Frank Carlson with his first-born son, Gerald (left) circa 1926. Frank Carlson with sons Richard and Gerald (right) circa 1928.

ing him, explaining that Richard was a baby and couldn't be expected to do things I could. That incident and his lying in his coffin are the only memories I have of my brother. I can still see the undertaker reach out and straighten the tiny fingers of Richard's right hand as he lay in his small, white casket in the living room of our home. I also remember going with my mother to Raiter's Hospital on Cloquet Avenue to pick up Richard's things. The few items—his sleepers, his security blanket with the blue satin binding, and a couple of toys—were bundled inside the Indian-print blanket that had covered him when he was carried into the hospital by our father several days earlier.

Richard had died on December 28, 1929, of measles complicated with pneumonia. He was seven days short of his second birthday. The Lutheran minister, Reverend Dahlen, and his wife, both properly garbed in mourning black, came to the house the day after the funeral (which I don't remember) and spent several hours praying and singing hymns. My mother was on her hands and knees scrubbing the kitchen floor when they arrived, and she didn't stop. After a particularly long, morbid dose of flat a cappella duet, she whispered to me loud enough so that they must have heard her, "I wish they would go!"

They didn't.

I'm certain the preacher and his wife thought they were helping my mother through her grief. Looking back, I can see where it would have been far better to let her work it out alone with the scrubbing brush.

Because the ground freezes solid to a depth of at least six feet during northern Minnesota winters, Richard's body was stored with the other winter dead in a stark, gray cement-block building at the cemetery until the spring thaw. This practice, of course, made it necessary for a family member to be present when the coffin was opened for positive identification of the deceased prior to interment. It also meant another funeral service at graveside and a renewed period of mourning for the survivors. It was almost as if a loved one died twice.

My mother never really got over losing Richard. I recall one time when I was well into my twenties and had done something of which she didn't approve. She stared straight through me and said, "I wonder what kind of a man your brother would have become." For an eerie moment, I had the impression that, to her, I embodied two people—my brother and myself.

Mom carried the ache of her loss in her heart all the way to her own death at age seventy-two.

My paternal grandparents are something of an enigma to me. I know quite a lot about them, but it is mostly bits and pieces, hearsay and gossip. I knew my grandfather as an old man of somewhat stocky build who tinkered in his blacksmith shop on Tenth Street north of Cloquet Avenue. He wore small, wire-rimmed glasses that rested solidly on the end of a slightly bulbous nose. He spent his summer evenings sitting on the porch of his home next door to his business playing out-of-tune classical music on either of his two clarinets (one ebony, one silver), a diversion that earned him the nickname "Beep-beep" from his near neighbors, some of whom were his own children and grandchildren.

The mailbox in front of grandfather's shop insisted in black, scrawled letters that his name was Nicolai Karlson. However, on legal documents such as his naturalization papers, the last name appears as Karlsson. As a young boy I could never understand how my grandfather could spell his name differently from ours and am still not certain why this was so. One theory has it that teachers changed the "K" to a "C" when his children were enrolled in public school. If that was the case, I assume they stole the extra "s," too.

My grandfather was born near the Russian frontier in northern Finland on December 6, 1859. Purportedly, his father was one Karlle Karlsson, a Swede-Finn, and his mother a full-blooded Finn whose first name was Katarine. Her surname and whether they had other children is unknown. Border skirmishes between Finns and the Russians, often with the sparse citizenry caught in the cross fire, were a continual thing. As a result, my grandfather was orphaned at age eight. Homeless and unwanted, he drifted southward from farm to farm begging and doing odd chores for food and a place to sleep. Once, in the dead of winter, searching for shelter, he was inadvertently locked in an icehouse overnight and nearly froze to death. Another time he slept too close to a fire and was severely burned on his arm and back when his clothes ignited. A sympathetic farmer's wife nursed him back to health. It's hard to imagine how he survived, given his age, but he said that he managed quite well as a wandering child, because even people in the poorest

Nicolai Karlson in his czar's army uniformat the time of the war with Turkey, 1877-1878.

straits rarely turned him away without a meal of some kind and a chance to spend a night in their barns. When he reached puberty, however, he suddenly found that whereas many lonely women on isolated farms were amenable to his presence, their husbands didn't want him around. At about age eighteen, he either joined or was conscripted into the Russian army and sent to the front to fight the Turks in the War of 1877-1878. A horse soldier, he told of troops dragging cannons by sheer manpower through deep mountain slows where more men perished on the pulling ropes from the cold than were killed in combat.

Nicolai Karlson remained a soldier in spirit to his death at age seventy-eight. At his request, he was buried with his two medals, a sharpshooter's decoration and a decoration for his being a member of the army band—these pinned prominently to his light blue Sunday suit. And considering what killed him, he should have had at least one other . . . but more on that later.

I knew my paternal grandmother, Marjana Mattila-Karlson, a little better than I knew her husband because she sometimes babysat me when I was very young. Born in Halsua, Finland, September 7, 1867, she was, as I remember her, a short woman, heavily wrinkled. In winter, her feet and legs were always encased in black felt boots that came up to her knees. A dark shawl covered her head in all seasons. She never learned to speak English.

Marjana Matilla-Karlson (circa 1888).

Marjana had arrived in America about 1888 in company with her father, a brother, and three sisters. Her mother had died in Finland when Marjana was sixteen years old. The family settled in Fitchburg, Massachusetts, where my grandmother operated a rooming house for "single ladies in the teaching profession." This concentration of females under one roof was soon sniffed out by my grandfather who had also turned up in Fitchburg in 1888.

Marjana was being courted by a blond young man, but dark-haired Nicolai got to her. As she told one of her daughters many years later, "That black bastard came at me like a bull!" She was raped and left pregnant in one brutal charge. With nowhere to turn, a single woman with child in the 1880s, Marjana married Nicolai in Fitchburg on April 13, 1889. I know nothing about the wedding ceremony, but I'll wager the father of the bride carried a weapon—a well-honed *puukko*, a deadly, decorative knife worn by Finnish men on formal occasions. Five months after the nuptials, a daughter was born, followed in quick succession by three more.

One of Marjana's sisters had married a John Nixonen shortly after arriving in America and had moved to Minnesota. Nixonen wrote my grandfather a hyperbolic letter describing the merits of the available farmland around a small community in Carlton County named Moose Lake. Nicolai soon had his again-pregnant wife and his four daughters ensconced in a two-story, four-room cabin in the logged-off, mosquito-infested swamps a few miles west of Moose Lake. All told, Marjana gave birth to fourteen big, healthy children (five girls, nine boys) and raised them almost singlehandedly. For most of twenty years she had one baby in her belly, one on her hip, and a third hanging on to her skirts. Every day during the summer months, she trundled a small wagon full of dirty diapers a half-mile to the shallow trickle of the Split Rock River to wash and then dragged them home again; in winter when their well surrendered to the freezing temperatures, she melted snow on the wood stove in the cabin. Except for the three children constantly with her, the rest ran wild in the brush like a pack of hungry young wolves. A favorite winter pastime for the boys was to see who could run barefoot the farthest through the snow before being compelled to seek the thawing relief of the cabin's stove.

Dirt poor, a new baby every year, the family survived on snared rabbits and what fish the boys could catch in the many lakes and streams, supplemented with whatever could be eked out of a garden wedged among the white pine stumps. A cow or two gave milk, which Marjana watered down to make it stretch. It's no wonder my grandmother once philosophized quite succinctly, "A stiff prick never looks in the bread box!"

Marjana's husband, Nicolai, was not a farmer. He often left my grandmother and kids on the home place while he moved about the countryside constructing barns, churches, and other contracted buildings. If he made much more than expenses, his family saw very little of it.

Mostly, I would guess, he just wanted to get away from the mess he'd created. Sometimes, if he could manage to corral one or two of the older boys, he took them along as unpaid laborers. Nicolai's absences were a time of relief and joy for all. On balmy summer nights, the girls would attend impromptu dances held on the wooden bridge spanning the Split Rock River between the home place and the then backwoods village of Kettle River. A number of Polish families resided in the area and someone always managed to come up with an accordion. Some of the pre- and early teen-aged Carlson boys often attended the dances with the sole purpose of starting glorious, no-holds-barred fights with "the Polacks."

When Nicolai was home, however, the good times ceased. Once, he hitched his wife and every child he could catch to a plow and then became enraged because they couldn't pull it. Unable to chase down the youngsters to vent his frustration, he savagely whipped my grandmother with a leather belt. In his final years, long after his wife had died, he vehemently denied that he was ever abusive; he said he was just "disciplining" as prescribed in the Bible.

Grandma Karlson was fiercely protective of her children, often taking beatings from her husband in their stead. In her eyes, they could do no wrong. When her ninth child, John, decided in the third grade that he'd had enough formal education and was caught shoving birch bark underneath the one-room country schoolhouse with the intention of burning it down, Marjana refused to believe it (John was asked to never return to the classroom, which suited him fine). Another time, after they were all grown, the police jailed a couple of the boys on a moonshining charge. There was no question about their guilt, but Marjana stormed into the Hotel Solem in Cloquet, complaining loudly and bitterly in Finnish to her daughter Lucy, "The goddamn cops have locked up my boys!" Lucy, the hotel's proprietress, bailed her brothers out.

Marjana Karlson died in a tiny, second-floor room at the Hotel Solem on September 20, 1932. She was sixty-five years old and had not been feeling well for several days. Lucy, well aware that her mother wouldn't get any rest or care around Nicolai, had taken her in to keep an eye on her. My folks and I lived in the house directly behind the hotel. When the undertaker finished his work, Marjana's body was brought to our place and laid out for viewing in the living room for a couple days as was the custom of the times. My bedroom on the second floor was directly over the bier. The first morning she was there, I sneaked downstairs in the half-light of dawn before anyone was up, tiptoed to the coffin, and looked in. Grandma lay on her back in the classic position. She wore a blue, flowered dress accented with a narrow white jabot. A string of dark-colored beads looped from behind her neck and rested on her breast. It is the only time I remember seeing her without a shawl covering her head.

As I stood there looking at her, I imagined I could see her breathing; her chest seemed to rise and fall ever so slightly. A thick smell of roses hung heavily in the room (to this day, the scent of roses reminds me of death). I reached out with one curious finger and touched her hand. It was like ice. Scampering back to bed, I pulled the blankets up around my ears and wondered what it would feel like to be dead.

I don't remember the funeral, but I do remember the ride to the cemetery. I cried all the way. I can also still hear the rocks bouncing on the pine box containing her coffin as her sons shoveled the earth into her grave, a stark finality to life spared the survivors in today's burial practices.

When the doctor was asked what had killed Marjana, he answered, "No one thing in particular. She was just worn out." Her last request, a plea really, was that she not be buried where her husband could be placed next to her. Forty-four years of his unceasing abuse had been enough. As a result, she lies alongside my brother Richard. When Nicolai died several years later, he was laid to rest next to his eldest son Alex on the opposite side of the cemetery. If Alex could have, I'm sure he would have picked up and moved!

2

The Town and the Folks

Change is inevitable. The Cloquet, Minnesota, in which I grew up does not exist today. This is how I remember it:

As one approached Cloquet from the east on State Highway 45, a small sign, black letters on white, posted on the right-hand shoulder of the paved road read:

CLOQUET
pop. 7,500

After crossing a pair of railroad tracks—a spur line to the toothpick factory on the left—the paved road became Cloquet Avenue. To the north and slightly east, the towering brick smokestack of the Weyerhaeusers' Northwest Paper Company jutted skyward like a Washington Monument with its corners rounded off. On days when the wood-chip digesters were being blown, one didn't have to look to know the mill was there. With an east wind, a goodly portion of the town's air turned rancid as the distinctive rotten-egg odor of sulfides permeated everything. The smell of prosperity.

The main street, Cloquet Avenue, ran roughly parallel two and a half to three-quarters of a mile from the mainline railroad tracks on the south bank of the St. Louis River. Ninth, Tenth, and Eleventh were the only streets that penetrated northward from the tracks. Bounded on the east by several acres of undeveloped, slate rock-burdened land and to the west by a huge lumberyard, the tiny three-street neighborhood formed a pocket of run-down houses, a small auto paint shop, a modest blacksmith shop, and, next to the railroad tracks, a half-dozen Standard Oil Company gasoline storage tanks. On the north side of the mineral-laden, root beer-colored St. Louis River, the land rose steeply to an elevation of several hundred feet. Forested with birch, maple, hazel, and green-barked "popple," a local name for a variety of aspen, the hillside became a profusion of reds and yellows of all possible hues in the fall season. At the top of the rise, the land leveled abruptly into fields of scattered farms. To the south of Cloquet Avenue, more gently sloped than the north side of the river, was the city's primary residential section.

Cloquet Avenue was the business artery of the community, both sides of the street lined with sundry commercial enterprises and public service institutions—to name a few: three or four gasoline stations, the Hotel Solem, the Leb Theater, the Dairy Inn ice cream parlor, several bars, the Tulip Shop cafe, Johnson Brothers' Hardware, a couple of auto dealerships, Raiters' Hospital, the Cloquet Fire Station, Jefferson Elementary School, two drugstores, several grocery outlets, the Shaw Memorial Library, the post office, and the Y.M.C.A., which died during the Great Depression for lack of funds or Christians or both and became the city-owned Civic Center—the usual services offered by any town of like size. Having covered eighteen blocks in reverse numerical order to First Street, the avenue jogged north for another block before continuing westward as Avenue C into a neighborhood of high-dollar homes populated primarily by professional people and top-level mill executives. Acting as a buffer between the elite and the railroad tracks were the City Hall, the police station, the bank, the Wright Hotel, and a number of small stores, shops, and offices. North of the tracks were the railroad depot and the Wood Conversion Company, which produced an insulation product with the brand name Balsam-Wool.

The citizens of Cloquet tended to group along ethnic lines, but rigid early-day divisions like Swede Town, Finn Town, and Blue Town had all but disappeared when I lived there. Perhaps the Great Fire of 1918 accelerated the integration process. An explosive forest conflagration, the fire engulfed huge portions of four abutting counties, killed 453 people, injured 2,100, and destroyed 4,089 homes as it consumed over 250,000 acres of property. It left little if anything standing in a dozen communities including Cloquet. One neighborhood, Little Canada, tucked behind Pinehurst Park and the cemetery and populated by descendants of early-day French voyageurs of the fur-trading era, was still close-knit in my time. Many of Little Canada's families sent their children to the parochial school run by Our Lady of the Sacred Heart Catholic Church (known locally as the French Catholic Church). Somewhat separated from the rest of us until they completed the eighth grade, enrollment in Cloquet High School quickly stirred them into the general milieu.

Northern Minnesota had four distinct seasons—not just winter and the Fourth of July as some claimed. Winter, given the state's latitude and not much between it and the North Pole except for a few strands of barbed wire, was the longest. For active young people, it afforded countless opportunities to experience the outdoors: skiing, ice skating, sledding, snowball fights, and sleigh rides. For the not-quite-so agile, the frozen lakes offered ample chances for ice fishing. The cold, sometimes dropping to thirty-five degrees below zero Fahrenheit, rarely stopped anyone. Neither did the snow. After a storm, city crews were out well before the general populace clearing and sanding streets and sidewalks to be ready for the early mass movements toward schools and jobs.

Summers were nice in spite of thunder-banging afternoon electrical storms, economy-sized mosquitoes, suffocating high humidity, and heat waves. The season did give folks a chance to tan their winter pallor, support the American Legion baseball team, and enjoy the many lakes for which Minnesota is famous.

Spring, while hailed by winter shut-ins, was not my favorite, especially early on, say April. The fields and lawns were all brown, their grasses flat to the soggy earth where they'd been compressed by the heavy winter's snows. Trees, except for scattered evergreens, were devoid of foliage, their bare branches silhouetted against gray skies like the hanging, bleached bones of murderers. The towns and hamlets were eerily quiet, their citizens still barricaded inside their duo-paned storm-windowed homes. Streets and sidewalks were gritty with accumulated layers of sand and gravel put down by those hard-working winter street crews. No, spring, especially April, was not my choice time of year.

Fall was my overwhelming favorite. Just enough snap in the air to be invigorating and to send the summer's crop of insects on their way to bugdom's Valhalla. Fall colors, crunchy leaves underfoot, the excitement of hunting preparations even if you didn't take part, high school football games, the homecoming snake dance—a winding line of hundreds of youths of all ages, hands joined, weaving through the indulgent community and ending at a huge bonfire with sparks shooting up into the starry sky. A short season—but the best!

The Daughters of the American Revolution was not a thriving social factor in our town. Most of the people residing in Cloquet during my youth were not far removed from their European roots. Almost all of my early boyhood friends had grandparents who immigrated to this country. At least two had parents who had been born in the Old World.

As offsprings of a mixed bag of northern European castoffs— Finns, Norwegians, Swedes, Danes, Poles, and Irish—we, as children, had few if any intercultural hang-ups. Ethnic backgrounds were rarely mentioned. I think the same applied to most of the adults in the community. They or their parents had left the Old Country to find a better life in America and very nearly cut all ties with their past. Most even gave up their native tongues, making no effort to teach their languages to their children.

The vanguard of the Norwegian immigrants seemed to cling the longest to bonds with their homeland. They had a hard time giving up their love of Norwegian royalty. Once, when I was about age four, the Norwegian crown prince passed through the community of Carlton about nine miles from Cloquet. He and his entourage were aboard a train bound from Minneapolis to Duluth. Norwegians flocked to Carlton from every point of compass, all but overwhelming the small community. Climbing telegraph poles, pushing and shoving for a spot where they could see the train, they watched and cheered as it passed, nonstop. Some claimed later to have glimpsed the prince in the windows of the royal car. While this was unlikely, for many the very thought of being so close to the crown verged on the orgiastic and kept the Norwegian Lutheran Ladies Aid a-twitter for days afterward.

The Finns, the largest ethnic group in the area, seemed to have cut the ties to their homeland as soon as they boarded the ships to come to America. Passionately independent and prone to unionism, they were considered "different" by many in the town. Some members of the Cloquet business community looked askance at the Finns because of their co-operative enterprises. At its peak in Cloquet, the Finn Co-operative operated two large stores, the Chevrolet dealership, a funeral home, a creamery, and had branches in several surrounding villages. Member-owned, they created what their detractors considered unfair competition. More than one disgruntled merchant chomped down heavily on his fat cigar and wheezed, "Communists!" under his breath whenever he thought about the co-ops.

Because they could work together, Finns had the reputation of being clannish. Stubborn, they fought forty-two wars with Russia and lost every one of them. Abandoned by their Swedish officers in the Battle of Viapori, the Finns fought to the last man—a Finnish Alamo. Czar Alexander I was so impressed with the Finns' bloody-nosed tenacity, he made Finland an autonomous grand duchy of Russia. It was, of course, a marriage doomed to eventual failure. The Russians' name for the Finns translates to "the unusual people."

Finns in America were sometimes accused of being atheists. While I'm certain there were some, I doubt the number exceeded that of any other ethnic group They did, however, have a healthy distrust of the clergy.

Suomi College in Hancock, Michigan, was founded in 1898 with funding from mining companies. Its avowed purpose was to turn out ministers to tend to the spiritual needs of the great influx of unattached Finnish men recruited to labor in Michigan's copper mines. The Finnish Lutheran Church had a long history of ingraciating themselves to management (mine owners and timber barons). Preachers were financed and encouraged by the power structure to repress union activity and keep labor in line. A great many of the hard-working Finns noted that the clerics expounding the merits of virtual servitude with rewards to come in the hereafter weren't getting any calluses on their own hands. They gave up the church and sought solace and companionship in the co-operatives and their social counterparts, the Finn Halls. Once the women who became their wives began to arrive on the scene and bear children, many families kept active in both the church and the Finn Halls.

When I was growing up in Cloquet in the 1930s, my friends and I kept an expectant eye on the Fourteenth Street Finn Hall. We watched for funerals, and when they occurred, we would attend the post-interment gatherings. It was no matter that we hadn't a clue as to who had died. The ladies of the hall always welcomed us and stacked our plates high with wholesome food and luscious desserts. For us, it wasn't a funeral. It was *Kahvi Aika*—coffee time!

The Swedes and the Danes were an integral part of the Scandinavian community but didn't seem to have the quirks— Norwegians' love of royalty or the Finns' co-op mentality. The Swedes and the Norwegians each had a Lutheran church on Carlton Avenue while the Danes, outnumbered on all sides, divided between them.

The Irish, predominantly Catholic, got along with almost everyone. As a slightly inebriated Norwegian once pointed out, "Irishmen are okay. See all that red hair and those blue eyes? They're just shipwrecked Vikings."

The Poles in Cloquet had their own St. Casimir's Church on Carlton Avenue and added another dash of spice to the potpourri of souls that gave the town its healthy diversity. It was my youthful observation that the Poles never took themselves too seriously. One of my wife's uncles, Henry Viakofski, who immigrated to America at age nineteen and worked for over forty years in the Cloquet paper mill, exemplified this character trait. He loved to claim with feigned seriousness that the Statue of Liberty, instead of holding the torch aloft, originally had an open right palm facing east. He also maintained that Emma Lazarus' first inscription on the statue's pedestal was an anguished plea: "Please, no more Polacks!"

There were, of course, people of other nationalities residing in and around Cloquet, a sprinkling from nearly every European country. Long Gypsy caravans of almost exclusively Packard automobiles, however, were always escorted through the city by the police and never allowed to stop. There were also the Indians.

Cloquet sits on the edge of the Fon du Lac Indian Reservation. Unfortunately, our contacts were few. I can only recall three students of Indian parentage attending school classes with me. We would see a few families on "Indian Payday" when they came to town with their government entitlement checks. They knew that their money was welcome even if they weren't. A majority of Cloquet's citizenry still harbored a frontier hostility toward Indians. It was, I feel, our loss.

3

Hans and Lucy

Hoping fervently that there was no other place like home, Lucy, the fourth of the fourteen Carlson children, was one of the first to leave the crowded cabin in the swamp west of Moose Lake. She chose to try her wings in Cloquet, a long day's journey by horse and buggy and train northeast from the home place.

Before its destruction in the Great Fire of 1918, Cloquet was a bustling lumber and logging center, a city whose air was heavy with the pungent odor of fresh-sawed white pine and punctuated by the incessant clacking of boards coming off the green chains. Its five sawmills employing great numbers of northern-European immigrants, many of whom were bachelors, the city was a coffer of irresistible enticements for a sixteen-year-old-going-on-thirty female with an insatiable drive to succeed.

Most of the unattached males resided in boardinghouses whose proprietors were always on the lookout for strong, naive young girls fresh off the farms who didn't object, and didn't know they could, to working sixteen to eighteen hours a day waiting tables, cleaning rooms, and scrubbing spittoons for a pittance. Lucy, trim and determined, raised around brothers and a lecherous father, was wise to the ways of men and could see opportunities beyond the ken of most of her contemporaries. Like her siblings still snaring rabbits on the farm near Moose Lake, Lucy cast about for a likely spot to catch a man, preferably one of means. She hired on at the Oswald House.

The Oswald House was one of the largest boarding establishments in Cloquet. The owner, A.K. Oswald, was a successful entrepreneur with fingers in several pies. He had taken on a protégé, a distant cousin from Norway named Hans Solem, and was teaching him the business from the bottom up. Hans was working as a cook when Mr. Oswald offered to sell him the business. Hans accepted.

Becoming the proprietor gave Hans more time and opportunity to lust after Lucy. He chased her persistently until she caught him. They were married in 1911. Lucy was eighteen years old, Hans thirty-two. The wedding, the social event of the season, was well attended by the upper crust of Cloquet society—the business community, politicians, mill executives, and the omnipotent potentates of the Sons of Norway. The bride's parents were not invited.

As it turned out, Hans Solem was a driver not a leader. He browbeat and abused his help, mostly women, until the day came when they quit en masse, leaving Hans and his wife to feed and care for ninety-six boarders. Although Hans probably never acknowledged it, like Lieutenant William Bligh, commander of His Majesty's Armed Vessel Bounty, the mutiny of his crew created Hans's eventual wherewithal. Lucy took over the reins of the business. Shrewd and energetic, Lucy laid down an ultimatum—Hans was to have no more direct contact with the hired help in any form. She and she alone would hire, fire, and supervise the staff. Any other arrangement and it was *jäähyvästi*, good-bye. It must have grated on the very core of Hans' Viking psyche, but he knuckled under.

The 1918 fire, blamed on sparks from trains igniting tinder-dry logging residue, destroyed the city but not the will of its people. Soldiers returning from the war in Europe found their hometown reduced to a collection of tar paper-covered shacks and a determined citizenry struggling to rebuild.

Hans Solem managed to get a seat on the city council and an inside track to fire relief money coming in from the state. With it, he and Lucy built the Hotel Solem on the ashes of the Oswald House. The new business thrived and, without any real competition, accumulated sizable profits over the years.

Lucy operated the hotel in accordance to the sweatshop standards of the day while Hans sat in an overstuffed leather chair at the back of the lobby and smoked his Havana cigars.

As a very young boy, I was aware that the Solems were my godparents and somehow construed that to mean that Hans was God. He looked the part. Living in the house directly behind the hotel, I must have walked past the large lobby windows ten thousand times and don't ever recall his not being there, a white-haired sovereign on a throne flanked by an enormous, highly polished brass spittoon, a cigar for a scepter. He could have died and no one would have noticed unless he dropped the cigar. Hans must have possessed a herculean urinary system. About the only time I ever saw him move was to chase my friends and me away from the hotel's dining room windows. A pack of incorrigible imps, we took great delight in flattening our noses against the large plate-glass windows fronting on Cloquet Avenue and, feigning starvation, tracking with sorrowful eyes every forkful of some diner's meal. My friends were just having fun; I was beginning a lifelong propensity for testing the tenets of religion.

Hans, the wrathful god, never connected me with the culprits annoying his guests. Partially blinded in an accident with a car battery, he couldn't see well enough to positively identify any single sinner in the fleeing group.

The Carlsons (circa 1912). Back row (left to right): Swen, Olga, Lucy, Nick, Ida, Alex, Hilda, Frank; front row: Alena, Charlie, Willie, Nicolai, Jalmer, Marjana, John, Oscar.

Sometime between 1910 and 1912, the ten or so Carlsons still on the farm west of Moose Lake, including Marjana and Nicolai, were forced off the land for failure to pay the taxes. They moved to Crosby, Minnesota, on the Cuyuna Iron Range where my grandfather and his two eldest sons, Alex and Nick, found jobs in the mines. My uncle Swen and my father, Frank, joined them in the diggings as soon as they reached their teens.

My father, barely fourteen, had been working underground for better than a year when he became ill. He lost a great deal of weight and was going downhill rapidly when Lucy came from Cloquet for a visit. She took one look at her younger brother's cadaverous appearance and insisted that he return with her to Cloquet. Years later, during a routine physical examination, a doctor asked my father when he'd had tuberculosis. Dad said it was news to him that he'd ever had the disease. Lucy probably saved his life when she talked him into quitting the mine.

Both Lucy and Hans had roving eyes. For years, Hans had a mistress living on Avenue F (poetic) whom he visited regularly while her husband was at work in the paper mill. Lucy's motto was, "Why keep one man happy when there are so many!" They apparently accepted each other's frailties and had been married fifty-four years when Hans finally dropped the cigar.

After Hans died, Lucy, possibly unwilling to face her own mortality, pulled out all the stops on her lifelong propensity for younger men and booze. (And Lucy could drink! Once, several years before Hans died, my wife Donna and I visited the Solems in Cloquet. I was twenty-eight years old and had some practice at holding my own with John Barleycorn. Lucy insisted that Donna and I join her and Hans on a round of the gin mills. Covering the county in the Solems' Cadillac, we hit most of the watering holes. Lucy tossed one whisky sour on top of another in a steady stream all afternoon, taking a break to "sober up" from time to time with a glass of strong beer. The designated driver and feeling no pain, I laid rubber on the roads as we moved from bar to bar. As the tires screamed, Lucy would squeal, "See, Hans! That's how young men do it!" Come evening, she was ready to go again. I couldn't move.)

An aged widow, alcoholic, obese, and bloated with booze, Lucy still managed to find plenty of young barflies willing to help her spend her money. One of them, in the course of a prolonged binge, hustled her off to Iowa away from the disapproving eyes of her two daughters and married her. A short time after the wedding, on December 30, 1966, at age seventy-three, she was dead. It has never been proven to everyone's satisfaction whether her husband beat her to death, or whether, in a drunken stupor, she fell in the bathroom and struck her head. The county coroner opted for the latter. Either way, the money her spouse gained from Lucy's death didn't do much for him. He died a year or two later of heart disease aggravated by acute alcoholism.

Hans and Lucy are buried together in the Cloquet Cemetery. When Hans died, Lucy had his grave site marked with an ostentatious headstone containing his name along with hers and a large, chiseled representation of the Hotel Solem. Their eldest daughter had the hotel ground off the stone soon after Lucy died. Hans's and Lucy's notoriety went with the dust of the removal. They simply became two names on a rock.

4

The Young Frank

My father was never a child in the usual sense. And he definitely wasn't ever a teen-ager from the mold in use today.

When his sister Lucy rescued Frank from the mine in Crosby and took him back to Cloquet, she put him to work in the Oswald House. He tended the furnace, hauled garbage, ran errands—the usual tasks wished upon a young gofer. One of his first memorable assignments was to thin out the cats.

Stray animals were attracted to the boardinghouse by the tantalizing odors of cooking wafting from the kitchen and the forbidden surreptitious feeding by kindhearted scullery maids. Hans Solem, obdurately opposed to extending the hand of charity to man or beast, ordered my father to get rid of them. He didn't say how.

Dad gave the problem some thought. The cats were numerous. Handling each one separately would be a long, gruesome operation. What he needed was some system of mass destruction, quick and humane. He put out some bait—table scraps and a couple of bowls of milk. When they had gathered, Dad counted twelve cats. Tying a dozen loose overhand knots in a length of clothesline, he slipped twelve heads into them. Fastening one end of the rope to a stanchion in the Oswald House's basement, he wrapped the other end around his waist like the anchor man on a tug-of-war team, and leaned back heavily. One dozen instantly broken necks. Gathering up both ends of the line, Dad tossed the whole works into the roaring furnace. The next day, Hans asked my father, "You making any headway on those cats?"

Dad answered, "Done."

Hans prowled about the basement and checked the garbage can area at the back of the boardinghouse. No cats. He shifted his cigar from one side of his mouth to the other a few times, a perplexed frown creased his forehead, but he never asked how.

20

Lucy insisted that her brother enroll in school. As a result, Frank was the only one of the fourteen Carlson children to graduate from the eighth grade.

Many of Cloquet's male population went off to work in the logging camps during the winter months. With the advent of spring and the accompanying break up of the ice on the waterways, they would follow the logs down the rivers to the mills and take jobs turning them into lumber until winter came around again.

Andrew Seim, a chef at the Oswald House, worked for the Solems during the summer months. Come winter, he, too, would move to the logging camps. My father, having no desire to continue on to high school, was hired by Chef Seim and went into the woods for one season as his second cook.

(The high school curriculum of the time wasn't likely to instill a burning desire for higher education in boys restless to be men:

First year—English readings, Latin grammar, rhetoric and composition, elementary algebra.

Second year—English readings, Caesar, physics, zoology and botany, plane geometry.

Third year—English literature, Caesar, general history, and physics.

Fourth year—English readings, Virgil, chemistry, physics, and mathematical review.)

Loggers lived in crowded barrack-like buildings reeking of body odors, drying sweat-soaked wool clothing, and stale tobacco smoke. Their employers, for the most part, considered them expendable chattel but refused to understand why unionism, especially the I.W.W., the "Wobblies," was becoming a problem. But loggers ate well. Even greedy timber barons realized that men working with two-man crosscut saws (known in the trade as "misery whips") and double-bitted axes in the cold from dawn 'til dark needed an abundance of food to keep going.

My father, along with Chef Seim and his family, lived in separate quarters attached to the mess hall. Dad's day started at 4:00 A.M. when he stirred the fires that had been banked all night in the huge cookstoves and ended when he rebanked them after the last clean-up of the evening. The Seims, Mr. and Mrs. and a couple of daughters, and my father ground out three Thanksgiving-like meals a day. Breakfasts and suppers were served in the mess hall, while lunches were taken out to the men working in the woods. Between meals, the kitchen crew cleaned, peeled, cooked and baked the massive piles of food it took to keep the loggers going.

Logging Camp No. 1 (top), Taft, Minnesota (circa 1915). Frank Carlson (bottom and standing on left), age fifteen, at Logging Camp No. 1 (circa 1915).

When spring rolled around and the men headed down the rivers with the winter's logs, the camp was closed. Chef Seim and my father returned to the Oswald House. Seim took over the kitchen from Hans Solem who had handled it during the slack winter months. Dad was reinstated as the resident gofer.

22

The winter in the woods with its hard work, good food, and fresh air apparently cured or at least arrested the tuberculosis my father didn't know he'd had. Sixteen years old, strong and healthy, he considered himself a man and above the menial tasks heaped on him by Hans and Lucy. He left the Oswald House and returned to Crosby.

Dad knew instinctively that he'd be wise to stay out of the mines. After a couple of weeks of visiting his family and friends, he and his brother John, who was a year younger, hopped a freight train to Wahpeton, North Dakota. They found jobs with a farmer who apparently admired their spunk and treated them almost as sons (years later, my father still spoke of the man with affection). The boys worked through to the end of the wheat harvest before returning home.

Wahpeton, a little over a hundred miles from Crosby, was just far enough to whet the boys' appetites for riding the rails. They'd met men working in the wheat harvest who'd painted pictures of fun and adventures waiting on the road. Back in Crosby, the two brothers and a friend, Oscar Yanka, decided to hop freights to Portland, Oregon. Arriving in the City of the Roses, they found jobs making barrels in a cooperage and wintered over in the St. John's area of the community. It was in Portland that my father joined his first labor organization. He carried an I.W.W. red card for a time. Although never active in union politics, he was a staunch member of trade unions all his life.

Riding the rails on their return trip to Minnesota the following spring, the three boys stopped in Dickinson, North Dakota, for food and water. Purchasing a few groceries, the three were hurrying to get back to the railroad yard before dark when they were stopped by the local marshal. The boys had been forewarned by other knights on the road to watch out for the law in the Dakotas. Many small town police had a good thing going arresting vagabonds as vagrants and then, with the aid of the justice of the peace, indenturing them for a price to unscrupulous wheat ranchers as unpaid convict laborers.

My father, having already backed down a railroad brakeman who wanted to throw the boys off a moving train in the wilds of Montana, refused to be detained. He told the paladin of the prairies to fuck off. The star packer went for his gun. He wasn't fast enough. Dad caught him flush on the button with a solid right, jamming his lower jawbone into the nerve centers under his ears and turning out his lights. Scooping up the unconscious officer's revolver from where it had fallen, Dad threw it side-arm down Dickinson's main street. The boys hid most of the night in brush near the train yards, managing to highball out on an early morning freight. As far as they could tell, no one searched for

23

them. Perhaps the marshal thought it wise not to let the townspeople know that a kid had put him away. Years later, my uncle John told me, "When Frank threw that six-gun, it skipped like a rock on a pond, kicking up sparks every time it hit the pavement."

The trio's luck ran out in Staples, Minnesota, forty-three miles from Crosby and home. Boarding a moving freight, John climbed aboard one car and my father, right behind him, caught the next. The train was accelerating rapidly and Dad, having difficulty getting on, tried to wave Oscar Yanka off. But the young man, eager to get home after his long absence, made the mistake of grabbing the ladder rungs at the rear of a car instead of the front. The train's momentum jerked him forward, whipping his legs and lower body backward between his boxcar and the one following. Losing his grip, he bounced off the coupling joining the cars and fell to the rails. My father jumped off the now racing train. Rolling on impact with the ground, he was unhurt except for a few minor bruises and abrasions. When the train had passed, he rushed to his friend's side. There was nothing he could do. The boy was still alive and partially conscious even though unknown numbers of boxcars and the caboose had cut through his midsection and lower legs. There was almost no bleeding—his severed blood vessels had been fused shut by the iron wheels.

Railroad section hands working in the area sent for a doctor, but Oscar Yanka died in my father's arms before the medic could get there. John, unaware of what had happened, continued on to Crosby alone. The victim's parents wired enough money to the authorities in Staples so my father could accompany their son's body home.

After Oscar Yanka's death, my father drifted back and forth between Cloquet and Crosby. He worked at the Oswald House and managed to pick up enough school credits to finish the eighth grade. He was in Crosby cutting and selling firewood when the Great Fire swept through Cloquet. The Oswald House was gone, the Hotel Solem an unrealized vision in Hans Solem's head, when World War I ended. At loose ends, my father, eighteen, signed a one year's enlistment in the U.S. Army.

Frank was not suited psychologically for a military life. He didn't take kindly to direct unchallengeable commands, especially those shouted at him. He detested jodhpurs-clad officers who slapped their swagger sticks against their highly-polished leather puttees as they strutted about with pompous airs of superiority. Brass whistles and Sam Browne belts irritated him, too—especially the whistles. "If they weren't yelling about something," Dad said, "they were whistling like a bunch of damned teapots." How he managed to complete his year and receive an honorable discharge is nearly beyond comprehension.

Shipped to Camp Grant, Illinois, the army put Frank to work in the stables. As my father said, "I liked horses. I just didn't like the horses' asses who rode them." If Dad and his stablemates received orders to have a certain horse saddled and ready to ride several days in advance, they took great delight in tripling the animal's oat ration. When the officer called for his steed, it would be as frisky as a mustang with a burr under its saddle. More than one chagrined dandy unceremoniously landed on his jodhpurs-encased backside when he attempted to mount a usually well-mannered horse.

On maneuvers in southern Illinois, Dad was assigned to drive a pair of mules pulling a wagon load of military equipment. When they bivouacked for the night, the mule skinners would usually ride their animals to the designated forage areas. One evening, Dad's mule

Private Frank Carlson (on the left), United States Army 1918-1919.

threw him. He landed hard and hurt his back. On returning to Camp Grant, he was still limping and went to sick call. The doctor said time would take care of the problem but insisted that Frank be relieved of shovel work in the stables. It was then that the army discovered he had cooking experience and put him in the kitchen. He worked as a cook for the remainder of his enlistment. Dad told me, "Leather-gaited whistle pricks rarely bothered the cooks."

I cannot recall my father every saying one good thing about military life. He hated it. I think he passed on his aversion to me, imprinted my subconscious. Maybe it's genetic. When I went into the U.S. Navy during World War II, the navy had a policy that any enlisted man who served twelve years with an unblemished conduct record was entitled to wear gold hash marks and rating insignia rather than red. Suffice to say, for now, that I blew my chance for gold less than six months into my military career. Like father, like son.

5

Beginnings: Part 2

My mother was baptized Elise Margrethe Christina Jorgensen. As was my father's, her name was also Americanized by the public school system to which she was known as Alice Margaret Jorgensen. Born in Catawba, Wisconsin, December 1, 1904, she was the fourth of five surviving children. Another five siblings died in infancy and are buried in forgotten, unmarked graves—one in Denmark, one in Elgin, Illinois, and three in Catawba.

I never knew my mother's father—my grandfather Jorgen Nielsen Jorgensen. The few photos of him that exist show a slim, mustachioed man with an air of nervous energy. One can almost hear him snapping, "Let's get this picture-taking over with. I have things to do!"

Like most men raised in the Old Country, Jorgen believed that as the male head of the household, despotic rule was his to administer as a God-given right. He failed, however, to reckon with the freedoms of America and greatly misjudged the inborn stubbornness of his brood. Those two oversights plus an inability to compromise eventually cost him his family.

Jorgen, his wife, nee Maren Kirstine Laurentine Jeppesen, and their first-born infant son, Charles, left Denmark under a cloud in 1898. A brick mason and building contractor, Jorgen had overextended himself on some construction projects when the world-wide economic panic of the 1890s crashed onto the scene. Unable to meet his obligations and too ashamed to face his creditors, he skipped the country with his wife and son and headed for America. Jorgen's overwhelming passion, verging on fanaticism, was to amass enough money so he could return to Denmark, settle his financial obligations and thereby again be able to hold his head high in his beloved mother country.

Kirstine Jeppsen-Jorgensen and Jorgen Jorgenson at their wedding, January 16, 1895.

In America, the Jorgensens first settled on the plains near Elgin, Illinois. A year later, lured by cheap land available in Wisconsin, Jorgen put fifteen dollars down on forty acres near the hamlet of Catawba. Loading the family—now numbering four with the addition of a newly-born daughter, Ella—a few sparse household items, a couple of cows, and other assorted livestock into a railroad cattle car, they headed north. The train had barely come to a stop on the siding in Catawba when Jorgen began a strict austerity program to reach financial solvency. In twenty years he built three substantial houses, two of which are still in excellent condition and are occupied today, constructed various outbuildings on neighboring properties, and established a reasonably thriving farm of his own. Of course, he didn't do it alone.

Maren Kirstine Laurentine Jeppesen was the product of a moderately well-to-do family on the Isle of Fyn, Denmark. Her father was a respected country postman and served as chairman of the Municipal Council of Gesteler Parish. He also farmed. The second of four Jeppesen sisters, Maren possessed that stubbornness and overt tenacity that had terrorized the Vikings' world for centuries and gave rise to the dreaded, foreboding cry, "The Danes are coming!"

A lithe, energetic, smallish woman, Maren worked extremely hard at her man's side in his quest to realize his dream. As time passed, however, she wasn't so sure she wanted to return to Denmark. As she learned English, she dropped the name Maren "because it sounded too much like a horse" and became Kirstine. She also began to question the justice in selling all the cream from their labors just to send the money to Denmark while the family drank skim milk, or why all the dollars from the building and selling of the houses went the way of the cream.

At least three of the five surviving children were way ahead of their mother in their realization that they were being shortchanged to pay the bills their father owed in a country about which they couldn't care less. Everyone worked. With Jorgen building, keeping the farm going fell to Kirstine and the children. Almost from the day the youngsters took their first steps, they were expected to help out with the chores—milking cows, tending chickens and geese, carrying water, cleaning barns, and handling the

Jorgensen children (circa 1909).

29

myriad of other endless tasks necessary to keep the system going. My mother, Alice, wasn't yet old enough to attend school when her father, in the process of clearing land, sent her to White's Store, a mile and a half walk from the farm, to purchase dynamite, caps, and fuses. The storekeeper put the explosives in a shoe box and warned her to be sure not to drop them on the way home.

As soon as they were able, Jorgen put his children to work outside the home place and confiscated their earnings. Charles, the eldest son, was sent to work in a logging camp north of Catawba. He was admonished to save his wages and bring them home to his father. And he did . . . for a time. The day was soon coming, however, when Charles, a young man enamored with the fashions sported by his peers, took his pay to the nearest town and spent it on a brown suit and shoes of the latest style. When Jorgen spotted his son proudly strutting in his finery up the lane toward home, he knew that Charles had spent his wages. Taking up his rifle in a fit of rage, Jorgen forced the young man at gun point to cover his sinful brown shoes with black boot polish and then ran him off the property. Charles never came back as long as his father was there. He quit his job, joined the U.S. Army and was soon on his way to France to save the world from the German kaiser. Let the old man try discussing the merits of brown shoes with General John "Blackjack" Pershing!

The other Jorgensen children in turn were also put to work to earn money for the bill collectors in Denmark. Ella, the second oldest child, was hired as a waitress at the Baker Hotel in Ladysmith, Wisconsin. She dutifully sent most of her earnings home. Thorvald, fourteen, looked up from his school desk one day to see his father talking quietly with his teacher. After Jorgen motioned his son outside he told him, "You've had enough school," and put him to work for a local logger. Thorvald stuck it out until he reached eighteen when he ran off and joined the U.S. Navy. At fourteen, my mother, Alice, was hired out as a housekeeper to a lady in Catawba. Independent to the core and inclined to be rebellious, my mother, well aware that her father would be waiting on payday to take her earnings when she arrived home, stopped off at White's Store. With Mrs. White's help, my mother made out a mail-order form for a new winter coat and sent it along with her wages to Sears-Roebuck in Chicago. Jorgen fumed and stormed, but the deed was done. In the future, however, he collected my mother's wages directly from her employer. Dagmar, the youngest of Jorgen's brood, wasn't yet old enough to work outside the home when the austerity program shattered beyond repair.

My grandfather should have foreseen trouble in his married life at its inception. His bride certainly made no effort to hide her independent nature from the beginning. For starters, she was a Baptist in a country smothered with Lutherans. And she refused to convert. As a result, she and Jorgen were married in a civil ceremony January 16, 1895, at the Odense Town Hall on the Isle Fyn. She did agree that any children resulting from the union would be brought up as Lutherans and followed through on the promise.

Then came the name change. Jorgen had married Maren and suddenly she was Kirstine. Unheard of!

As his kids began to figure out which direction down the road led to town and not bring home their wages, Jorgen's austerity program began to show ominous cracks. Farming his children out for cash left all the chores at home for him and Kirstine. No doubt they were both worn out from years of excessive labor. He'd bitch at her, which he should have known was the wrong tack to take with a headstrong woman. She'd snap back. He'd push. She'd push back. He'd storm. She'd throw a tizzy. They were in the barn when it ended. She was sick of his austerity bullshit and said so. He told her to remember that he was the master of the house. It has never been recorded just exactly what she said in reply, but Jorgen grabbed Kirstine by the neck and shoved her face into a fresh cow pie. By the time Kirstine got all the manure out of her facial orifices and was able to breathe again, Jorgen was gone. He was never seen by any of his family again.

The split took place in 1920. Nothing was heard of or from Jorgen until early in the 1930s when word came from some thirdhand source in Europe that he'd died in Denmark. His family wrote him off without visible tears or fanfare. Then, shortly after New Year's Day 1949, my mother received a letter postmarked December 28, 1948, from Copenhagen. It was from her father.

The letter was a maudlin note to "My lovely little girl." It went on to say, "I am getting old and good for nothing. Now I have to die very soon. You know I am eighty-five now but Father is with me. You may not understand that when you and I was together I was so awful busy so I never had much time [to] learn you anything about Father but He is and He will be, and He is with me now." The letter closed with, "Dear little Elise, if you can come here I will give you the nicest coat you can find in the store."

My mother never answered the letter. Her only comment was, "He wasn't around when I needed a father. I don't need him now!"

My grandmother, Kirstine, when told that her exhusband was still alive in Denmark, snorted, "Humph! He was supposed to have died a long time ago. He can stay dead."

(When I began the research on my family history in the 1980s, I chanced to locate a very distant relative, a Mr. Svend Bohn in Copenhagen, who was able to fill in some of the blanks concerning my grandfather Jorgen Nielsen Jorgensen: Jorgen was born February 23, 1864. He was authorized as a bricklayer July 25, 1889, by the Bricklayers' Union in Odense, Isle Fyn. He worked three years on a job constructing a castle for some crown prince in Germany. He returned to Denmark upon finishing the project and set up the contracting business that eventually failed in the panic. After skipping out on his family in Wisconsin, he took up his old trade and was in the Tacoma area of the state of Washington for a time. He returned to Denmark in 1923, paid off his remaining debts, and worked at his brick mason trade until he retired at age sixty-seven. Active in the Salvation Army before emigrating from Denmark, he resumed his affiliation with the organization on his return. He died in Copenhagen December 28, 1949—exactly one year after the postmark on his letter to my mother.

Kirstine legally divorced Jorgen in 1921. She never remarried. Neither did he).

6

Moonshine

Completing his one-year enlistment in the United States Army, my father drifted back to Cloquet. He went to work for Hans and Lucy as a cook in their newly-built Hotel Solem—the Waldorf-Astoria of Cloquet at the time. He'd been there nearly two years when Lucy hired a young waitress, a pretty, sixteen-year-old Danish girl from Catawba, Wisconsin. She was strawberry blonde with just enough freckles to be interesting, and she caught Frank's eye. Her name was Alice Jorgensen. She had freckles on her, but . . . she was cute!

Alice had come to Cloquet with her younger sister Dagmar and their mother Kirstine. The mother had sold the farm in Catawba soon after her husband had taken off for parts unknown. Kirstine's sons, Charles and Thorvald, on completing their military obligations, had found jobs in the lumber industry in Cloquet. Although the Great Fire

Alice Jorgensen-Carlson, age sixteen (circa 1920).

33

of 1918 had all but destroyed the city, several sawmills located on Dunlap Island in the St. Louis River had survived and were processing logs floated downstream on the river's tributaries from as far as 128 miles to the north. Kirstine and her daughters settled into a house on the southwest corner of Avenue F and Tenth Street. Unwilling to accept financial support from her sons, Kirstine hung out her shingle as a seamstress.

The Jorgensens, except for my mother, didn't stay long in Cloquet. The Nash Motor Company had begun opening new plants in Kenosha, Wisconsin, and the Jorgensen boys, attracted by the work available, decided to move. Kirstine, with her youngest daughter in tow, followed them. Alice, by this time in love with Frank, stayed behind. (The move by the Jorgensens tended to separate my mother, and eventually me, from that side of my family. There were, of course, occasional visits back and forth, but they were of short duration. The result was that I never got to know my mother's people as intimately as I would have liked.)

My parents had a whirlwind courtship. They met at the Hotel Solem in late summer 1921 and were married in Carlton, Minnesota, the county seat, on January 24, 1922, during their break between lunch and dinner at the hotel. Considering that it was an eighteen-mile round trip between Cloquet and Carlton, and taking into account the time it took to pick up a license, locate a minister, and have the marriage performed, they must have given new meaning to the term "quickie."

Shortly after they were married, Dad took his bride to Crosby to meet his folks and those of his siblings who were still there.

My grandfather Nicolai, referred to by his children as simply the old man (most often preceded by earthy adjectives), had quit the mines and opened a blacksmith shop. Apparently, it was not a successful enterprise in and of itself; but, the Eighteenth Amendment to the U.S. Constitution—the Volstead Act of 1919—had made it economically feasible. When Dad took Mom to the shop behind his folk's house in Crosby, they found the old man climbing up from a tunnel beneath the floor. The tunnel led to a small still.

(Coming from a strict law-abiding Danish-Lutheran background dedicated to the tenets of teetotalism—unless Jorgen could be faulted for taking to sipping vanilla extract in symbolic defiance of government-mandated sobriety—my mother could hardly believe the family she had married into. She couldn't know it at the time, of course, but later, when she and my father brought me from Michigan to Minnesota, she was to be caught up in the covert intrigues of illicit booze operations for several years. Mom must have loved my father desperately to stay the course when the very idea of lawlessness was abhorrent to her . . . at first. She eventually adapted and accepted what was to be rather than fight it.)

While the old man made moonshine in his cave in Crosby, his sons—Alex, Nick, and sometimes the younger John—would run it into Superior, Wisconsin, a wide-open lakeport city that welcomed loggers, sailors, and miners and knew how to keep them coming back.

Running whisky had its risks. There was, as one would expect, the law which necessitated cat-and-mouse maneuvering to avoid the police every time a delivery was made. But even more disconcerting was the threat of being hijacked by rival bootleggers, an event that, unlike a simple police arrest, had the potential to erupt into shooting warfare. One night Alex and Nick were making a run to Superior when, just east of Aitkin, Minnesota, their car's feeble magnetoelectric headlights picked out a telephone pole—a naked pole without crossarms or wires—laying across the highway. Unwilling to stop, Alex kicked in the low-gear pedal of their Model T, hopped the high-centered Ford over the barrier, and sped on. Nick thought he had heard a single gunshot over the clatter of the rapidly accelerating engine, but there were no bullet holes in the car when they arrived in Superior.

Another time, unable to wring enough alcohol out of the old man's still to meet the demand, Alex, Nick, and John visited a farmer who they knew was dabbling in moonshine. The farmer agreed to let them have five gallons but said he would have to go to his cache for it. Instructing the brothers to wait in their car, he drove off in his own rig. The three had to wait quite a while under the watchful eyes of the farmer's wife, whom they could see peeking at them from behind her curtains. The man finally returned, money and booze changed hands, and my uncles headed for Superior.

John had little more than a second grade education, but he was shrewd and possessed uncanny animal instincts. As they made their way down the road, John spotted the recent tire marks where a vehicle had been parked off to the side. On a hunch, he had Alex stop and quickly tracked his way to the bootlegger's hoard about a mile off the road in dense woods. Needless to say, the brothers cleaned out the store.

In the meantime, the farmer-bootlegger got to musing about the three customers he had just serviced and decided to visit his cache again. He arrived on the scene just as my uncles pulled away.

Much agitated but unwilling to chase after three men by himself, the man hurried back to his farm and phoned the sheriff. He couldn't very well say that the brothers had stolen his moonshine, so he reported that they had robbed him of his money. He had failed to get their license plate number but passed on their physical descriptions.

Alex was driving when the three crossed the state line into Wisconsin. Approaching the outskirts of Superior, the boys were congratulating themselves on their successful coup when the law in the form of a city police car full of officers seemingly appeared out of nowhere behind them. Alex opted to ignore the flashing red light and the screaming siren. The chase was on. The police, under the impression that they were in hot pursuit of armed robbers, opened fire. One bullet drilled through the rear window of their target, whistled past Alex's right ear, and smashed on through the windshield. Alex brought the car to an abrupt halt. The brothers climbed out with their hands high.

Once the initial hubbub subsided and my uncles convinced the police that they were unarmed and hadn't done anything except stumble upon some illegal whisky hidden in the woods, more practical heads came to the fore. The officers, some of Superior's finest, weren't really interested in enforcing the prohibition laws nor were they adverse to supplementing their incomes if the opportunity arose. They confiscated the fifty-three gallons of booze in question and sent the brothers on their way.

Although my father didn't actually become involved with moonshine—except, no doubt, as a consumer—until we returned to Minnesota from Michigan in 1926, he did get sentenced to sixty days on the St. Louis County work farm one week after marrying my mother in 1922. His brother Alex had passed through Cloquet on his way to make a delivery—he kept changing routes between Crosby and Superior for obvious reasons—and Dad, with a day off from the hotel, decided to ride along. As luck would have it, he and Alex were stopped by the police in the suburb of West Duluth. Charged with transporting fifty gallons of whisky, they served a third of their time and were released.

Before we left Michigan, my father had already decided that he was going to emulate the old man but on a much grander scale. As my uncle Jalmer, the youngest of the fourteen Carlson children, told me years later when I asked him where Dad had learned to make moonshine, "Frank was the only one of us kids to get through the eighth grade. He could read. He picked up a book somewhere that learned him how to make good whisky and just followed the directions." Dad must have studied that book well; one of his distillery enterprises destroyed by Carlton County Sheriff Selmer Swanson's "Purity Squad" was hailed in the newspapers as "the largest operation of its kind in the State of Minnesota." Jalmer, after an extensive amount of research, averred to his dying day that he "never tasted better booze than the stuff Frank made."

I have a lot of very vague memories of those early bootlegging days. Some may not be memories at all but stories I heard after the facts. The passing of years has made it hard to differentiate in some cases. I know that we lived in a number of different houses in and around Cloquet. We owned a series of large, beautiful automobiles. My folks hosted numerous parties with lots of dancing (on visiting one of the houses in later years, I found that the china chandelier in the dining area still had the scars of missing chips purportedly nicked out by the heels of one of Dad's partners when he swung her high). Frank and his brothers seemed to come and go a great deal at night; they had stills cooking at various locations throughout the forests of both Carlton and St. Louis counties.

Like any successful businessman, my father believed in reinvesting in his company—updating his equipment, improving his product, and expanding his market. This meant going into bigger and better stills, charred-oak aging barrels, and enlarging the overall area of distributions. It wasn't long before Dad and his brothers were running booze all over northern Minnesota and as far south as Menomonie, Wisconsin.

The ever-vigilant Purity Squad suspected that the Carlsons were in the moonshine business, but catching them wasn't easy. They could hide whisky better than any squirrel stashing nuts. One house we lived in had a large pile of winter coal in the backyard. By moving a few pieces of the black stuff and then pulling a hidden pin, it was possible, with minimal effort, to shunt the entire pile aside and expose a storage pit. On two different raids, the police came with warrants and, in the process of searching, poked around that coal pile without success. Local deliveries of a gallon or less were often handled by one of Dad's teen-aged nephews, his sister Hilda's son Clarence. In broad daylight, Clarence would walk down Cloquet Avenue with a transparent gallon jug clearly labeled KEROSENE but containing colorless moonshine. Surveillance officers never gave him a second look.

Although I was much too young to have an active role in the shenanigans swirling around the Prohibition Amendment, I wasn't entirely left out. I remember accompanying my father on a ride to

Duluth. We drove to a huge warehouse on the waterfront of Lake Superior. Inside, the building was divided into stalls, much like the stalls in a horse barn but much larger. Instead of housing horses, however, the compartments were heaped high with unlabeled clear-glass bottles: half pints, pints, quarts, magnums, and gallons. The place was crowded with men and a sprinkling of women, all buying and paying cash for empty bottles. I didn't exactly understand what it was all about but realized later that all those people were bootleggers and the building was a bottle-supply house, the bottles having come into Duluth on Great Lakes boats from Toledo, Ohio.

Along with an invaluable education in the wiles involved in the carrying out of human endeavors, I did manage to reap some tangible benefits from the prohibition era. A couple of years ago, one of my lifelong friends told me, "I always looked forward to visiting at your house when we were little kids. You had so many neat toys."

It was true. Dad gave me every toy I considered a childhood necessity. I don't remember receiving the first walker he bought for me, but I reportedly rode it down the basement steps and whacked my head on the concrete floor. I'd been scooting around the kitchen when Dad, not thinking, left the basement door open. His reaction, once he decided I wasn't dead, was as to be expected. He smashed the walker into pieces, not admitting that he was the one who forgot to shut the door. Once I quit howling about my bruised head, I wanted my walker. Seeing it was ruined (and I do remember looking at the wreck—the walker was painted blue with white trim), I set up another howl and didn't stop until my father went out and purchased a new one.

The walker was followed by a succession of pedal cars, tricycles, scooters, and wagons. I apparently loved anything with wheels. Now, at sixty-plus years, I'm not so enamored with machines as I am with going where they can take me.

Surprisingly, none of the Carlson clan ever did any major prison time in all the years they were in the whisky business. Public opinion, except for some preachers and other assorted bluenoses, was on the side of the bootleggers. The vast majority of the country's citizens resented any legislation governing their personal drinking habits. Given that climate, a great many law enforcement officers were ready and willing to look the other way for a "consideration." One successful aspirant to the office of Carlton County Sheriff was said to have declared to friends, "Give me two terms, and I'll retire to Florida a rich man." And he did.

The few times family members went to jail, they didn't stay long. Once John was picked up during a raid on one of my father's stills in neighboring St. Louis County. He was sentenced to the work farm and assigned to a road gang. He was there less than a week when his brother Swen drove his Model A Ford along the road where John was filling chuckholes. Swen slowed as he passed, and John slipped into the back seat, lay on the floor out of sight and escaped. Swen took his brother to Cloquet where John picked up his own Ford coupe and headed west. He spent the winter in Portland, Oregon. When he returned to Cloquet the following spring, the law had already given up its halfhearted search for him.

My father was charged with operating an illegal still in 1929 and sentenced to five months in the St. Louis County Jail in Duluth. Dad always covered his tracks well, but someone had noted that he was purchasing large amounts of sugar, far more than the local bakeries, and reported it to the authorities. Following up on the tip, the Purity Squad surprised Dad at one of his stills. Sure enough, he wasn't turning out cookies.

Frank only served about a month of his sentence. Mom, with two babies (my brother Richard and me) in tow, went to the judge and said she had no way to manage with her husband, the children's father, in jail. As if on cue (no, I don't think I was coached), I blubbered, "I want my daddy!" Richard, seeing me crying, set up an accompanying howl.

His honor, a compassionate man with a bright red, purple-veined nose, realized that with Dad's incarceration his own dwindling private stock was being replenished with whisky of inferior quality. He suspended my father's sentence.

Another time, Dad was tripped up when he sold a bottle of whisky to a sheriff's informer in Carlton County. He hired a local attorney, Jerry Baron, who knew the Carlsons well. The day the case went to court, Mr. Baron instructed my father and Dad's brother Nick (they were strikingly similar in spite of a couple years' spread in their ages) to dress in identical clothing. The stool pigeon, under oath, couldn't swear for certain which brother had sold him the spirits. The judge threw the case out of court.

My father's oldest sister, Ida, was the only girl in the family to do jail time for dealing in moonshine. Her tenure in the business was extremely short, but she was incarcerated for a longer period than any of her brothers ever were for the same offense—giving credence to George Bernard Shaw's observation that pilfering a loaf of bread could get a thief a life sentence whereas stealing a railroad would guarantee him a seat in the House of Lords. But more on Ida later.

7

The Wright Hotel

Although I was only about four years old when my folks purchased the Wright Hotel in Cloquet and pushing six when we left, I have fond memories of it. A two-story structure with horizontal wood siding built sometime after the Great Fire of 1918, the hotel has had many roles over the years: a hotel, purported house of ill repute, and an apartment complex, but it was still a hotel when my parents owned it. I learned to cuss masterfully there, an ability that has, on occasion, served me well.

The Wright Hotel was not in the same class as the Hotel Solem. The Solems catered to a soi-disant, genteel, main-street clientele—corporate mill executives in town on business, traveling salesmen, a number of spinster schoolteachers—whereas the Wright Hotel was a working man's haven located next to the Great Northern Railroad Company's tracks.

Wall Street in New York was sucking in its breath for its infamous dive and the Great Depression was just around the corner when we moved in. The establishment catered almost exclusively to railroad men. A continuous stream of ore trains—we called them ore-jammers—passed through Cloquet on their daily runs between the Mesabi Iron Range and the lakeport cities of Duluth and Superior. This activity, along with shipments of raw materials and goods in and out of the paper mill, the wallboard plant (later known as the Wood Conversion), and the toothpick factory, created a need for a sizable contingent of track laborers and other railroad personnel, a number of whom chose to reside more or less permanently at the Wright Hotel.

Many of the railroad men were without close family ties, and I soon became their surrogate nephew of sorts. There was an illegal slot machine (owned by a concessionaire on good terms with the law) in the hotel's lobby. Along with broadening my vocabulary, the trainmen soon taught me the relative advantages of cherries over lemons as they let me feed their nickels into the one-armed bandit and pull the handle. They also introduced me to rolling the bones and the accompanying jargon of inveterate dice players. Little Fever, Little Joe, Boxcars, and Snake Eyes were indelibly imprinted in my young, receptive brain. Daydreaming in my first grade arithmetic class one day, the teacher jerked me back into the real world with, "Gerald, what is three plus two?" Jarred from my reverie, I answered, "Little Fever!" She looked at me rather strangely. Recovering quickly, I said, "I mean five."

The teacher, probably chalking me off as another weird kid, continued her lesson without comment. I wonder what would have transpired had she asked me the sum of two plus one and I'd answered, "Crap!"

It was at the Wright Hotel that I became acutely aware for the first time that there was some mysterious difference between men and women that went beyond the obvious fact that the latter wore dresses while the former favored trousers.

There was a woman living in the house next door to the hotel who had the disquieting habit of preparing for bed each night without lowering her window shades. The hotel guest who had the room directly across the narrow alleyway from the lady's boudoir discovered this nightly exhibition and couldn't keep it to himself. Suddenly, each evening about 9:00 P.M., the men lounging in the lobby after a hard day's work would energetically transform into a frenetic mob as word was passed that the show had begun. The lobby would empty as if to the sound of a fire alarm as a dozen or so men jammed into a single, darkened room, shoving and jockeying for viewing space at the lone window.

I was never allowed to join the men—Mom's orders. The nightly stampede continued for several days. Then, without warning, the lady ruined it all by religiously drawing her blinds forevermore. I have a strong suspicion that my mother had something to do with the woman's new found modesty. The morning of the day she drew her shades, I had noted her and Mom having a quiet conversation in the backyard.

I witnessed my first real bar-busting brawl at the Wright Hotel. I don't remember what the occasion was, but all the furniture in the lobby had been shoved to the walls and a big dance was in progress to the music of a small, fiddle-and-kick country band dominated by a loud, if not well-played, accordion. There was quite a lot of traffic between dance numbers as people went back and forth to their cars. This soon led to a lot of shiny eyes, flushed faces, and general merriment.

My uncle Willie was holding down his usual position in the stag line, looking the girls over and trying to dredge up enough nerve to ask some young lady to dance. Willie was extremely shy around the opposite sex, and as often happens to men like that, he tended to go for the bottle and its false courage. Unfortunately, when Willie drank, he quickly forgot about the swirling skirts on the dance floor and turned into a disputatious drunk. Harsh words passed between him and some other fellow. The first punch was thrown. A woman screamed. A chair or two were knocked over, and the whole place exploded into a glorious free-for-all.

My mother, prepared for the usual grand finale of most moonshine-infused country dances, calmly ushered my teen-aged cousin Lillian and me into a room just off the dance floor where we were quickly joined by several frightened, excited young women. Climbing onto a chair for a better view over the heads of the females hogging the doorway, I witnessed one of the greatest Donnybrooks ever to take place within the city limits of Cloquet. Much of the battle is but a blur in my memory today—a combination of the real event and some of the saloon-wrecking brawls depicted in the never-missed Saturday matinee westerns at the Leb Theater (admission: five cents or an empty Arco coffee can). One picture, however, stands out vividly: My father, a big, bloody grin on his face, has some guy down in the middle of the dance floor and is methodically punching his lights out. He seems oblivious of his sister Lucy who, skirts up to her crotch, has him straddled and is vainly trying to pull him off his victim by strangling him with his own necktie.

The back door leading to the garage behind the hotel was one of those old-style models with a heavy, bevel-edged window making up the top two-thirds of it. Somebody knocked a man by the name of Allie Gamble right through it, leaving him wasted in a pile of shattered glass on the steps outside. Mr. Gamble was a gentleman if not a successful brawler. He came around the next morning, albeit a little worse for wear, and paid my mother for the damage.

I was four months short of my fifth birthday when I was packed off to Miss Ann Visanko's morning kindergarten class at Jefferson Public School between Eighth and Ninth Streets on Cloquiet Avenue. My mother escorted me into a big room with a lot of little chairs arranged in a large circle supplemented by some low risers tucked into a small alcove. It seemed there were kids everywhere (our class picture shows forty-one) hanging onto their mothers' skirts and screaming pitifully for them not to leave. Others, abandoned to the risers or the little chairs, were reduced to sobbing, howling, snotty-nosed wrecks.

My mother sat me on one of the little chairs, said a few words to the harried Miss Visanko, and left. I waited quietly, took in the bedlam and asked myself in good railroadese, "What the goddamhell are these kids yowling about?"

Besides whacking two sticks together to lend rhythm to "The Glow Worm" as a reluctant member of The Tiny Band, there is one other thing I remember learning in kindergarten: You cannot walk to the Cloquet Golf Course by way of the Great Northern Railroad's tracks. I know because I tried.

I sometimes straggled back and forth to school with another morning kindergartner named Delbert Golen who lived near the Wright Hotel. One Indian summer's noon as we moved west along Cloquet Avenue toward home, Del said, "We can make a lot of money if we go to the golf course and find lost golf balls." We could see the green ridge in the distance where we supposed the golf links to be. It appeared as though the railroad tracks ran to the very edge of the fairway.

Well aware that my folks would never consent to let me walk the tracks no matter how profitable the venture might be, I decided to negate their objections by simply not asking them.

Because the railroad tracks veered away from the town just beyond the Wright Hotel, we had no choice but to pass in front of the lobby's windows to get to them. Mom always had my lunch ready and watched for my return from school, allowing some leeway for four-year-old meandering. To escape detection, Del and I edged in next to the building and, creeping on all fours, slipped past virtually under my mother's nose.

Once out of the line of sight from the windows, we ran to the tracks and headed for the distant golf course—our Eldorado. We walked and walked, stepping off the tracks from time to time to let the steady stream of ore-jammers zip past at seventy per on their downgrade run to Duluth and Superior. The engineers of the huge steam-propelled locomotives usually returned our waves, some with quizzical expressions on their faces as they pondered about why two small boys would be so far from human habitation. We crossed two long, curving trestles spanning the mineral-darkened waters of the St. Louis River, stopping each time to listen for approaching trains before skipping from tie to tie as fast as our short legs would go.

Time passed quickly. Almost before we realized it, the sun was riding low in the afternoon sky, its rays barely penetrating the surrounding woods that cast long shadows across the track line. By this time, we realized that we didn't have any idea where the golf course was located, but, firm in our belief that we must be close, we pushed on. Finally, we heard a railroad speeder coming from the direction of Cloquet. In a few seconds the little yellow machine with one man on board stopped behind us. The man seemed surprised to find us there and asked where we thought we were going. We told him. He insisted that there was no golf course the way we were headed and suggested we'd better be getting home. Warning us to watch out for trains, he continued on his way.

It was a long hike back. We were tired, thirsty, and hungry. I finally spotted the hotel in the distance, its windows reflecting the last rays of sundown, a beacon of hope. We were hurrying our steps, anticipating the welcoming succor of family and food, when I saw her. Skirts flapping in no-nonsense fashion, my mother, immensely relieved (I think) and more furious than I'd ever seen her, charged up the tracks to meet us. She had a stick in her hand, not a switch but a good thick stick, and she used it first on me and then on Del Golen. When she finished with Del, she pointed him toward his house and started on me again. I got a lick about every third step all the way into the kitchen of the hotel where she sat me down to my now cold lunch that had waited since noon.

I was blubbering and crying, trying to impress her with all the wealth I had planned to acquire at the golf course, when my father walked in. The whole town had been alerted to look for us, and preparations were being made to drag likely spots in the river. Dad asked where we had been and listened calmly to my hiccuppy story. When I finished, he went into the bathroom and returned with his razor strop. Pulling down my pants, he bent me over his knee, doubled the strop on itself, and whopped my bottom four or five good licks. He didn't really hurt me, but the pop of that doubled-over leather made me believe I was being murdered. It was the only time my father ever spanked me—mostly because I made damned sure he never caught me at anything that would have required a repeat performance.

While I wasn't an active participant in the learning experience, another lesson that came my way at the Wright Hotel was: Never use a kerosene stove to warm a cold automobile.

One winter's morning as I sat at the kitchen table dawdling over my oatmeal and considering ways to get out of going to school, my father stepped outside to check the thermometer tacked onto the garage's wall. He was only gone a minute when he came back looking frozen and announced that the temperature was thirty-five degrees below zero. He needed to use his brand-new 1929 Dodge that day (probably something to do with his moonshine operation), but this was long before the advent of multiple-temperature lubricants and the oil in the car's crankcase had the approximate consistency of frozen molasses.

Not to be deterred, Dad rounded up a three-burner kerosene stove and headed back to the unheated garage. He fired up the burners and slipped the unit under the Dodge's oil pan. It had been his practice to stay with the car until the oil liquefied to where he could start the engine. But this time the garage was exceptionally cold, and he dashed back into the warm kitchen, thawing his frozen fingers on a hot coffee cup while he waited. He didn't stay long, not more than six or seven minutes, before braving the elements and returning to his project.

Dad had hardly left before he was back again. I can see him in my mind's eye as clearly as if it happened yesterday: He stood in the open kitchen doorway, the cold air vaporizing in billows around him, stared unbelievingly at my mother and said, "The goddamned thing's burnt up!"

And it was. Dripping oil or grease must have ignited, and the Dodge went up in smoke. All the wiring, the mohair upholstery, and the tires had burned away. The beautiful, new sedan was reduced to a smoldering hulk. The strange thing was that the gasoline tank never exploded and the garage didn't catch fire. But the car was a total loss.

No, there wasn't any insurance. Wall Street had started to crumble, the mines up north were cutting back which led to economy measures for the railroads and empty rooms at the Wright Hotel. Dad, who never believed in insurance anyway, had let the policy on the Dodge lapse two weeks before the car incinerated.

8

Alex

We were still in the Wright Hotel when my uncle Alex shot and killed a man in Missoula, Montana.

Alex Carlson (circa 1930).

Alex was enamored of the West. I don't know if he was attracted by the wide-open spaces or by the wide-openness of the gambling fraternity. Because of his fondness, verging on addiction, for cards and other games of chance, I suspect it was mostly the latter.

(About a year after Alex's death, I happened into my uncle Nick's room and found him marking a deck of cards by blending small, unobtrusive dots into the design on their backs. He confided that he and Alex, on occasion, had supplemented their mine wages in Crosby with such devices. I decided then and there that if they could cheat like that, anybody could. I've shied away from gambling ever since.)

Alex's first trip west was in October 1918, less than one month before the armistice ending World War I. He and Nick received their draft notices the same day. Alex promptly tore his into shreds and announced emphatically that he "wasn't going into any goddamn army just because a bunch of fat-assed bankers got their balls into a vise in Europe." On October 19, 1918, as Nick patriotically reported for induction at Brainerd, Minnesota, Alex shouldered a pack sack and hopped a freight train headed toward the Rocky Mountains. Three months later, Nick was honorably discharged at Camp Dodge, Iowa, and returned to Crosby. Alex, learning that Nick was home from the service (they were close buddies besides being brothers), bummed his way back from Montana where he'd been working on a cattle ranch. The two brothers again took jobs in the iron mines until the advent of Prohibition when they began running booze for the old man. No one ever made any effort to prosecute Alex for evading the draft. Perhaps his transgression was overlooked in the turmoil of the Great Fire, the killer flu epidemic that swept across Europe and America, and the euphoria of the war's end.

In the process of delivering moonshine to Superior, Alex became friendly with a lady bootlegger and brothel operator known affectionately as Shotgun Hilda, a moniker she acquired in the course of terminating an unhappy marriage (she hired a good lawyer and was found innocent by reason of self-defense).

Changing men, however, did not alter Shotgun Hilda's basic hair-trigger temperament, and she and Alex had a turbulent relationship at best. Alex was handsome and mostly easygoing. He believed in enjoying life, which, for him, meant women and gambling—easy come, easy go. His favorite quote, which mirrored his intrinsic philosophy of life, was: "Work is for horses, and even they turn their asses to it." Shotgun Hilda was Alex's antithesis—querulous, ambitious, and close with a dollar. They warred constantly.

Whenever the battles became too much of a burden, Alex would take off for the West until things cooled down. If the cards were good to him, he'd return decked out in flashy Hollywood cowboy duds and riding a Pullman. If, as was more often the case, the cards failed to cooperate, he'd slip into Superior on a freight train and charm his way back into his lady's graces.

Alex's last trip west might not have occurred except for my father's punching ability. It was a warm, sunny afternoon and a bunch of the Carlson's were socializing in the yard at their sister Ida's shack on the lower end of Tenth Street in Cloquet. Ida's husband, Henry "Hakey" Aho, an affable Finn, who had a crock of home brew working continually but almost always "sampled" it out of existence before any of it ever got bottled, was hosting the event, a sort of wine-tasting party without the benefit of grape products. The festivities were just warming up when Alex's car ground down the hill in a cloud of dust and flying gravel. Alex was obviously agitated, a sure sign his lady was on the warpath again. Ten minutes later another automobile came roaring into view with Shotgun Hilda at the wheel.

Alex, trapped on a dead-end road, took off running across backyards toward Eleventh Street and points east. Shotgun Hilda jumped out of her vehicle, a .32 Smith and Wesson revolver in hand, and took up pursuit, screaming after her fleeing lover that she was going to "blow his philandering ass off." Concentrating on her target and looking neither left nor right, she failed to notice my father move into position to intercept her. As she charged past, he caught her with a solid right hook to the jaw. As my uncle John put it, "She flipped ass end over tea kettle."

When Shotgun Hilda finally regained consciousness, the fight was out of her, and she headed meekly back to Superior. Dad gave the revolver to Alex who had returned to the party after his lady left. The next day he headed west.

Alex sort of evaporated into the sunset, and no one heard anything from him for better than a year. Then, one day out of the blue, my aunt Lucy was making the rounds of the family, taking up a collection to hire an attorney to defend him on a murder charge.

I didn't learn any of the details of the killing until I took it upon myself to look into the matter fifty-five years after the fact. Between court records and a running account in *The Missoulan* newspapers of the time, here, briefly, is what happened:

Late Friday night or early Saturday morning, June 14 or 15, 1929, a man named Carl Saari was killed in the Western Hotel in Missoula by a single .32 caliber bullet that entered his abdomen and skittered willy-nilly through his intestines before coming to rest in a muscle of his hip. According to the accounts, Alex and the victim had been employees of the Heron Lumber Company west of Arlee, Montana. The two men checked into the Western Hotel about 9:00 P.M., Friday, June 14 and were assigned room 30 on the third floor. Around midnight, the desk clerk, Richard Duell, found Saari lying in the hallway outside the room the men had rented. In his testimony, Duell said he could smell alcohol on the man and assumed he was in a drunken stupor. He dragged Saari into the room and dumped him on the bed.

The next day about noon another hotel employee, Mrs. Olga Bonnes, entered room 30 to make it up and found Saari on the floor dead. Because there was no blood in evidence, it was assumed the man had died as a result of consuming the contents of two partially emptied Mason jars containing alcohol, one found on the floor near the body, the other on the bed. When the coroner, undertaker John Forkenbrock, was summoned, however, he soon discovered the bullet wound. An autopsy performed by Drs. C.L. Bordeau and J.J. Flynn ascertained that death had resulted from internal bleeding.

Alex maintained that while he and Saari were drinking, Saari had asked him to participate in an armed robbery. Alex refused and Saari turned ugly, storming out of the room. Returning a short time later, Saari found the door to room 30 blocked from the inside by a chair wedged under the doorknob. Alex insisted in court that he had barricaded the door because Saari was fighting drunk and armed with a razor. He also claimed to have witnessed Saari use a knife on a man on another occasion and had no doubt that Saari would kill him if he got back into the room. Alex further testified that he considered jumping out of the room's single window, but the three-story drop dissuaded him. He then took his .32 Smith and Wesson from his pack, sat on the edge of the bed, and waited as Saari, shouting death threats and obscenities, kicked the door. When the door began to give, Alex squeezed off two quick shots. One bullet embedded itself in the wall next to the door while the other passed through the door itself.

Alex said all ruckus ceased with the gunfire. He waited ten minutes or so before opening the door and found Saari lying in the hall where Mr. Duell eventually came upon him. Alex grabbed his pack and fled, leaving the revolver on the third step down from the third floor landing as he ran. Police were never able to locate the weapon.

Alex's attorney, E.C. Mulroney, entered a plea of self-defense on behalf of his client when the case went to trial July 8, 1929, in District Court, Missoula, Judge Theodore Lentz presiding. The door to room 30 with its single bullet hole was brought into the courtroom as evidence. The doctors who performed the autopsy on the deceased testified that it wasn't unusual in a wound such as Saari's for all bleeding to be internal thus collaborating Mr. Duell's contention that he saw nothing to alert him that the man had been shot. Defense attorney Mulroney brought forth police records that showed Mr. Saari had a long history of arrests for fighting and public drunkenness in Missoula and capped his presentation with a maudlin plea to the jury to remember that Alex was a friendless stranger far from home and family.

After four hours of deliberation the next day, the jury of twelve men found Alex not guilty.

The reporter or reporters assigned to cover the case for *The Missoulan* made an issue of the fact that both Alex and Saari were Finns from Minnesota. (Carl Saari supposedly came from Cracow, Minnesota, but authorities were unable to locate any town by that name or any of his relatives. Sarri was buried in potter's field in Missoula.) In direct quotes attributed to Alex, they wrote what they must have assumed was a northern Minnesota-Finnish dialect; but it comes out like the French-Canadian patois of the dog-mushing mail carriers in Jack London's *The Call of the Wild*. At least one reporter seemed piqued that Alex was acquitted. Perhaps he had been looking forward to attending a hanging.

According to *The Missoulan*, Alex left their city the day following his exoneration, headed for St. Maries, Idaho, to "mek goot money in de voots."

Until they sent him back in a box, Alex never again returned to Cloquet or Superior. He had drifted away from his old ties and, besides, had he returned, someone might have asked to be reimbursed for his attorney's fees. On May 16, 1934, at age thirty-nine, Alex was killed in an automobile accident near Nyssa, Oregon. According to Oregon authorities, Alex was working in a logging camp out of Nyssa when he came down with severe food poisoning. He was loaded into the back seat of a car that failed to negotiate a tight curve on a mountain road en route to a hospital. Two other occupants in the vehicle escaped with minor injuries, but Alex died instantly of a broken neck. Because he was working for wages at the time of his death, it's a sure thing that the cards had been going against him. He left the world as he came into it—flat broke.

Lucy, determined that her brother wasn't going to be buried a stranger far from family, again made the rounds of the siblings, raising funds to transport Alex's body to Cloquet. She met some resistance from brothers who considered it a waste of money to bring him to a town he had never considered his home, but she persevered, and the Nyssa undertaker received a Western Union money order. Times being what they were in 1934, the mortician must have gone a little mad at the sight of cold cash. He jammed Alex's large frame, clad only in long underwear, into a small coffin and shipped it on the first train out.

Tommy Meraw, a longtime, respected Cloquet funeral director, claimed the body when it arrived. He reshaped Alex's nose which had been flattened by the coffin's lid, straightened out his jammed-up legs, and dressed him in a first-class cut-down-the-back burial suit. Even dead, Alex was one of the most handsome men in a family of handsome men.

The only thing I remember about the funeral is the small scandal that erupted. Two teen-aged girls, Shotgun Hilda's daughter and a friend, showed up with an enormous wreath. You'd have thought Alex carried the winning jockey in the Belmont Stakes from the size of it. But, what caused the horrified tongue-flapping among Alex's sisters and smirks of delight among his brothers was the wreath's satin ribbon. In large gold letters it read: FATHER.

Alex had never married Shotgun Hilda, and her daughter had been born before she killed her husband. . . .

(I saw Shotgun Hilda in Cloquet several years after Alex's demise. My mother pointed her out to me while we were shopping for groceries. It appeared that the passing of time had not been kind to her. She looked tired. Somewhere along the line, her nose had been broken and never straightened properly.

Many years later, in the course of gathering material for this book, my wife, Donna, said she remembered a Shotgun Hilda living near her grandmother's place west of Cloquet. Donna never saw the lady but said she and all her childhood friends always hurried past Shotgun Hilda's house like kids taking a shortcut through a cemetery on a dark night. They had heard that Shotgun Hilda had killed a man and feared that she might shoot them.)

My uncle Swen gave Alex a final unwritten epitaph. When Lucy came around again, this time seeking a donation for Alex's tombstone, he dismissed her with, "Tombstone? Hell, a slot machine would be more like it!"

9

Tenth Street

What with the uninsured Dodge going up in smoke, the lack of paying guests at the Wright Hotel due to the advent of the Great Depression, the loss of his stills to the Purity Squad with resulting lawyers' fees, fines, and his short incarceration (thanks to Mom), Dad was, as they say today, having a "cash flow" problem. Putting it in context with the times, he was flat-ass broke, and we were out of the hotel business. We moved to North Tenth Street.

I don't know what my folks paid for the house behind the Hotel Solem, but it couldn't have been much. At first glance, again by today's standards, it should have been condemned and used for a fire-fighting exercise. Two stories high, the building sat on a half-lot covered with weeds, some over six feet tall. If the horizontal wood siding on the outside of the building had ever been painted, there was no evidence of it. Out back was a decrepit one-holer heaped to the brim, but the piece de resistance was the refuse disposal system; the previous tenants had simply thrown all their garbage upstairs.

I think my father was intrigued with the challenge the house represented. In the six years or so that we owned the place, he put a full basement under it, completely refurbished the interior with bright wallpaper and paint, installed indoor plumbing, built a two-car garage, and turned the dump into a respectable home.

(Underneath all the squalor, structurally, the house must have been sound. It still stands today—a modest, comfortable home wedged between the parking lot of the Hotel Solem and Ruben Liimatainen's Hardware Store.)

Living on North Tenth Street was absolutely kid heaven. Our whole world consisted of three dead-end streets—Ninth, Tenth, and Eleventh—extending downhill from Cloquet Avenue and terminating at the railroad tracks. A half mile or so beyond the tracks, the beer-colored waters of the St. Louis River, impeded by the Minnesota Power Company's dam, moved sluggishly on its way to Lake Superior. To the west of Ninth Street was a large lumber-drying acreage and several huge horse barns. (When the Great Fire of 1918 destroyed Cloquet, fourteen saloons and several sawmills on Dunlap Island in the St. Louis River somehow survived. The stands of white pine that nurtured the mills were, however, reduced to ashes. A couple of the sawmills hung on for a few years but eventually folded for lack of raw materials. Only one continued to operate until the advent of the Great Depression. It was this remaining company that stacked fresh-sawed lumber on the acreage and kept draft horses—huge breeds of Belgians, Percherons, and Clydesdales—in the large, white, curb-roofed barns fronting on Ninth Street. Awed by the magnificent beasts, almost every afternoon I trotted my six-year-old legs through the alley behind Raiter Brothers' Hospital to watch the beautiful animals prance on their enormous hoofs to their stalls at the end of their workday.)

To the east of Eleventh Street was another large acreage known as Kallio's or Little Woods, a vast undeveloped place of hazelnut and chokecherry bushes scattered among substantial outcroppings of fractured slate, that was an ideal setting for playing cowboys and partaking in various forms of childhood mischief. (A family by the name of Kallio once had a home on the property, but, except for some crumbling remnants of a cement foundation, it had disappeared before my time.)

In retrospect, the three-street neighborhood, isolated from the rest of the town on three sides, was a mini version of New York City's Hell's Kitchen, a kind of ghetto populated primarily by the financially destitute and lots and lots of kids. Ninth Street was home to uncountable numbers of Heikkalas, Kincaids, Peterses, and Ahlgrens, all loosely led by a tough kid named Sulu Heikkala. On Tenth Street, the bailiwick of the Ericksons, Batters, Ahos, Edwards, Bodins, Lackeys, and myself, we independently shunned recognition of any single leader. Eleventh Street was the turf of the Arbuckles, Deans, Merfields, Hagens, Matsons, Sunnarborgs, and Bodins (the same Bodins as listed on Tenth Street; they lived next to the railroad tracks halfway between their two streets and their allegiance could go either way depending on the situation).

For the most part, we were a peaceful lot, which allowed for great summer ball games and the usual wintertime activities. On those inevitable occasions when disputes did arise, the parties involved usually settled them individually (Jerry Merfield and I had a running battle of unknown origin for years; evenly matched, neither of us ever managed a decisive victory). Once in a great while, because all three streets were graveled, fights would deteriorate into rock-throwing melees. Many years after I left Cloquet, Sulu Heikkala came to visit her sister who happened to reside in the same West Coast city that I do. She asked him if he'd like to drop in on me and renew acquaintances. Sulu thought for a minute and said, "I don't know . . . he might throw rocks at me!"

      I smoked my first tobacco shortly after moving to Tenth Street. Willard Bodin, a boy with a faulty tear duct in one eye which gave him the appearance of being on the verge of crying all the time, had acquired a pipe and a lead-foil package of Peerless tobacco. He and my cousins, Violet and Evelyn Aho, were in the alley (really just a path running between back-to-back outhouses) that separated Tenth and Eleventh Street properties. They were daring each other to be the first to partake of Willard's illicit goods when I wandered onto the scene. Younger than the others, I was, in my eagerness to be accepted in the new neighborhood, a pigeon ripe for exploitation. I did my duty. Regrettably, instead of getting sick I rather liked the encounter and was started on the road to an addiction that lasted some twenty-five years.

Gerald Carlson and Melvin "Bozo" Erickson (circa 1937).

On the plus side, I credit my juvenile butt-sniping days to the fact that I still have all my teeth. Neither of my parents smoked, forcing me to become an oral hygiene maniac in an effort to cover my tell-tale breath.

      My best friend in those early days was Melvin "Bozo" Erickson. He was my age and lived with his parents and a flock of sisters across the street and down a couple of houses. We were inseparable. We were incorrigible. We once launched a misbegotten endeavor to bilk the local Ben Franklin five and ten cents store.

      The "Dime Store" on Cloquet Avenue was about two doors west of the Hotel Solem. What lured Bozo and me into trouble were the barrels of penny candy— jelly beans, licorice drops, Walnettos, peanut butter kisses—lined up in bulk along one wall of the store. We worked ourselves into a sweet crave and decided to try our hand at filching from those tempting open casks. It must have been a Saturday or Indian payday on the Fon du Lac Reservation west of town because the store was crowded when we made our move.

Bozo and I, each standing about belt high to an average man, squeezed our way through the crowds of shoppers to the barrels. Pretending to contemplate on the various selections of candy, we wedged in among several ladies and, out of sight of the few clerks, grabbed two handfuls apiece from four different choices. Jamming the loot into our pockets, we nonchalantly exited the way we had entered.

Success! Parking our thieving little rears on the curb in front of the Hotel Solem, we made short work of our ill-gotten goods.

But our criminal master stroke had just whetted Bozo's appetite. His triumph had bred contempt for caution. I, on the other hand, was having second thoughts about being a thief. I had a gut feeling that another pass through the store would be a disaster. Bozo set off to do it alone.

I was still sitting on the curb wondering if I hadn't been over-cautious by not joining in the second caper when the calm of Cloquet Avenue was shattered by bloodcurdling screams for mercy. I watched as Mr. Harnish, the store's proprietor, burst out of his establishment, pulling a howling Bozo along by his left ear. I tried to look as angelic as possible as they hurried past me. Mr. Harnish hesitated for a second as our eyes met, but the sun reflecting off of my halo must have convinced him of my purity. He continued on with the business of delivering Bozo to Mrs. Erickson and justice.

Bozo didn't squeal on me as I knew he wouldn't, and I swore off shoplifting for life. Bozo, of course, received a memorable whipping from his mother, but that was the expected and easiest part of his punishment. His mother belonged to a fundamentalist, evangelical church whose members were known locally as the Holy Rollers. He was condemned to a long term of praying, public confession, and endless church services.

Of course, Bozo and I weren't the only thieves on the block. One respected businessman, a staunch member of the Norwegian Lutheran church who passed the collection plate each Sunday, operated a store next to the Hotel Solem for years. His storage basement was connected to the hotel's. Hans Solem was always complaining that he couldn't keep light bulbs in his subterranean laundry and storage areas, and he accused his help of pilfering them. Not so. As a little kid wandering around the hotel's basement one day, I saw the pious shopkeeper remove several light bulbs from their sockets and slip back to his own storage area. I told my mother what I'd seen. She told Hans, but he scoffed at my story. The accused, after all, was a fellow businessman, a pillar of the Norwegian church, and a staunch member of the Sons of Norway—ipso facto, I didn't know what I was talking about.

Today, most youngsters' heroes are comic strip characters or members of rock groups. Ours were bank robbers. We followed the careers and exploits of John Dillinger, Babyface Nelson, Homer Van Meter, Machine Gun Kelly, Pretty Boy Floyd, Bonnie and Clyde, the Baker-Karpis gang, and others. And we weren't alone. Banks and bankers were not popular during the Great Depression. Grown-ups and kids alike, watching the newsreels in the Leb Theater, would cheer and applaud when images of Dillinger and other gangsters were flashed on the screen, and then boo and hiss when arresting officers and prosecutors were shown. We practically went into mourning when Dillinger was gunned down in front of the Biograph Theater in Chicago by FBI agents under command of G-man Melvin Purvis.

Shortly after Dillinger's death, the Post-Toasties cereal company came up with a box-top promotion encouraging kids to send away for a genuine Melvin Purvis badge and become members of the Junior FBI. In our neighborhood the effort was a complete flop. If any kid sent for G-man Purvis's tin star, he didn't tell anybody. Post-Toasties would have done a lot better offering replicas of Dillinger's famous wooden gun.

Of course, our hero worship spilled over into our play. We spent at least one entire summer in an ongoing game of robbers-and-robbers (nobody wanted to be cops for cops-and-robbers). Our weapons were rubber guns. A rubber gun—I haven't seen one in years—was simply a board cut in the shape of an elongated Colt automatic with two spring-type clothespins fastened to the back of the handle. Rubber rings cut from old tire inner tubes were knotted in the middle and stretched from the weapon's muzzle to the clothespin triggers. Before the summer was over, every kid in the neighborhood carried a brace of two-shot side arms from dawn 'til dusk. A few of the older boys also packed ten-shot, rapid-fire machine guns (shaped roughly like rifles, notches cut into the "barrels" held the stretched inner tube rubbers which were anchored over a length of heavy string or sash cord; one pull of the string sent all ten missiles flying toward their target at once). If a player was shot, he lost his weapons to his antagonist and had to acquire new guns from his fellow gang members so he could go after the dirty rat who got him. It was a memorable season of ambushes and pitched gang battles unencumbered by adult rules and supervision.

In spite of the general air of criminality in our hero worship and play, I know of only one kid from the three streets who ever had serious trouble with the law. He must have been about fourteen or so when he used a hatchet on a local shoemaker in a robbery attempt. Fortunately, the victim survived, although badly wounded. The boy was sent to the state reform school in Red Wing, Minnesota, his family moved away, and I never heard of him again.

The country's economic woes that had helped to drive us out of the Wright Hotel worsened as the Great Depression deepened. Adamant in his refusal to apply for public assistance, universally known as "relief," my father started a blind pig operation in our house.

Normally, Dad stayed clear of blind pigs; too many people became aware of what was going on and that inevitably led to police raids. But the failure of the Wright Hotel on the heels of the loss of his distilling operations to Sheriff Swanson's Purity Squad had left him few choices. He began purchasing booze in five-gallon quantities from wholesalers and pushing it out by the drink or the bottle in our kitchen.

I liked the blind pig. I met a lot of people I would have missed otherwise—Pine River Tony (a bachelor who lived in a shack on the bank of the Pine River north of Cloquet and subsisted on moonshine, muskrats, and beans), Step-and-a-Half (a wispy little man with one leg considerably shorter than the other, the result of a logging accident in his youth), Dirty-Neck Mary (a lady who, like the courtiers during the reign of Louis XIV, powdered instead of bathed; curious, I once sneaked a peek at the back of her neck—it was dirty), Grasshopper Gloria (her Finnish given name translated to the insect in English), and a host of others. They'd show up at all hours but mostly in the early morning to get their start on the day. I'd pretend I was a bellboy—the "Call for Phillip Morris" cigarette ad was big on the radio at the time—politely answer the door and usher customers to a seat at our table. A few blinked the first time they ran into me but had overpowering needs that superseded any piddling intrusion into their lives. Most were hurting and shaking so badly they couldn't get a shot glass to their lips without spilling it—they'd leave the glass on the table and go down to it—and considered me just another irritant on their way to temporary wellness.

Dad would also make the rounds to the country dances on Saturday nights, his waistband tucked with pint bottles of moonshine for sale. Once in a while, Mom and I would go along for the ride. One evening, we arrived at the Chub Lake Pavilion near Carlton, Minnesota, just as a big fight started on the dance floor. People were bailing out the windows to the sounds of breaking furniture and loud cursing. As we sat in our car taking it all in, one of our regulars, Step-and-a-Half, limped from the building and, spotting us, hobbled over. "Frank," he pleaded, "You got a gun? Lemme borrow your gun."

"I don't have a gun," Dad answered.

"Dammit to hell!" Step-and-a-Half swore as he moved off. "I need to kill that sonofabitch!"

Step-and-a-Half apparently failed in his search for a weapon. He was behind our door the next morning as usual with nothing but his eye-opener of the day on his mind.

Upstairs in the hallway leading to my room in our house on Tenth Street, Dad had a secret storage place for moonshine behind a sliding panel in the wall. I wasn't supposed to know about it, but one day on my way to my room, I surprised him just as he opened the cache. It was heady stuff for a seven-year-old, a hideaway behind a false wall just like in the "Charlie Chan" and "Fu Man Chu" movies at the Leb Theater. Dad showed me how it worked, told me it was our secret and swore me to silence (a vow I've kept—until now).

My mother, of course, abhorred the blind pig, so it wasn't in operation very long. When it ceased, I knew without anyone telling me that Dad had his stills going again.

The U.S. Congress officially ended Prohibition on December 5, 1933. Individual states then ratified the repeal at their own speed— some almost immediately while a few others, mostly in the Bible Belt of the Deep South, stalled for up to thirty years.

Although I was only eight years old, I clearly remember the spring day in 1934 when booze became legal in Minnesota. We had a big party in our backyard on Tenth Street. Marv O'Hearn, preparing for the grand opening of his new bar on Cloquet Avenue, had been selling chances on pony kegs of beer for weeks. My father won one. Halfway through the afternoon, the keg was empty, the hat was passed, and the group purchased a larger, standard-sized replacement. I remember everyone saying the new beer would never replace home-brew quality. Having done considerable sipping from adults' glasses throughout the afternoon, I concurred. Be that as it may, Prohibition

Prohibition ends in Minnesota, 1934.

was finished. My father and his brothers buried their copper stills somewhere in the wilderness in St. Louis County. Our moonshining days were over.

(Those copper stills are still waiting out there. Someday, someone is going to dig up some great antiques.)

10

Saints and Sinners

I must have been in the second grade at Jefferson Elementary School when the last sawmill in Cloquet quietly closed, and the beautiful horses and their barns disappeared.

I was one of the few who bemoaned their passing. By this time, Cloquet's economic base had changed. After the Great Fire had burned away the slash left from the logging era, white birch and a fast-growing variety of poplar trees ("popple" to us natives) with green-colored bark took over the landscape and became the raw material for a match and toothpick factory, a wallboard plant, and a paper mill.

The Depression years were tough in Cloquet as elsewhere. There were cutbacks, even in the new industries, and unemployment was high. Men accustomed to earning their living in the logging camps had to face the double trauma of losing their outdoor jobs with the end of the timber supplies and then seeking nonexistent employment in factories. It drove a lot of good men to drink.

Boozers and their problems were considered commonplace facts of life to all us kids living north of Cloquet Avenue. With the ending of Prohibition, I don't know what Cloquet had more of—bars or churches, but I do know we had an excess of both. Drunks would stagger off Cloquet Avenue, and gravity would draw them downhill through our neighborhood until they crawled in somewhere or ended up in the hobo jungle along the railroad tracks at the bottom of the slope.

Most of the inebriates moved through quietly and received scant notice by the community, but there were exceptions. One time a bunch of us were playing in the lumberyard west of Ninth Street (the lumber piles were great for king of the hill or just plain jumping off into the years' accumulations of sawdust and chips that covered the ground) when two police cars sped into the area followed by a half-dozen or so civilians on foot. We, of course, immediately thought we were in big trouble for playing there and had visions of being on our way to Red Wing, the city of the dreaded state reform school. It turned out, however, that some old fellow with a drinking problem had become "snakey" (the accepted colloquialism for the delirium tremens) and, unnoticed by us, had climbed on top of one of the lumber piles to escape the slithering, scaly horde only he could see. Armed with a hefty plank, he flailed the vipers as they squirmed over the top edge of his sanctuary, making it extremely hard to get him down. The police shooed us out of there, so we didn't see the end of the episode.

Most of the victims of delirium tremens weren't so violent. They saw different things—rats spiders, and even monkeys. At least a couple I observed saw nothing unusual. They just became traffic policemen in their own minds. More than once, I watched some inebriate stand in the middle of Cloquet Avenue waving his arms about as he "directed" traffic until the police would come by and take him away.

One of the business enterprises on Cloquet Avenue was Dube's Tavern and Boardinghouse. Most of the guests were single men who lived there more or less permanently. Dube and his staff looked after them. One evening an elderly Norwegian named Ole was sitting in the lobby long past his usual early retirement hour. Mr. Dube knew that Ole had been hitting the bottle and asked, "Up kind of late aren't you, Ole?"

"Yah," Ole replied.

"Why don't you go on up to bed?" Dube suggested.

"Can't," answered Ole.

"Why not?" questioned Dube.

"My room's full of monkeys," Ole answered matter of factly.

"Monkeys?" Mr. Dube asked, a glimmer of realization of what was up reaching him. "What kind of monkeys?"

"All kinds," Ole insisted. "Big ones, little ones, all kinds."

"Aw, Ole," Mr. Dube said as he moved toward the telephone on the lobby wall, "you're not afraid of monkeys."

"Only the biggest one," Ole replied. "He sits on the end of my bed, and that would be all right except, by Yasis, he talks Norwegian to me!"

Once in a great while, ill and lonely, some poor man in a solitary room somewhere in the city would hang himself.

Almost all the churches in Cloquet were located uphill from Cloquet Avenue as if to be closer to heaven. There was a bunch: Finnish Lutheran, Swedish Lutheran, Norwegian Lutheran, Polish

Catholic, French Catholic, Presbyterian, Pentecostal this, and Evangelical that. The only thing missing was a synagogue although there were two or three Jewish families in town.

Competition for souls among the churches was not great because each congregation was made up primarily of a single, cohesive ethnic group. There was, however, a minor undercurrent of suspicion and distrust between some of the Catholics and Protestants, mostly confined to a few bigoted preachers and the busybody types who tend to dominate small-town religious activities.

My mother, raised Danish-Lutheran, was forced to pick another church in Cloquet as there was no Danish congregation. She chose the Norwegian church. For what reason, I never bothered to find out. Dad wasn't interested. Neither were any of his siblings. In their own family they'd observed the hypocrisy of their father, the old man, holding the Bible in one hand while laying a leather strap on their mother with the other. My father's brother John, when asked once what he wanted done with his remains when he died, sort of summed it up for the majority. He answered, "Bury me face down. That way the snakes will have a home."

I, of course, was dragged off to the Norwegian Lutheran Church by Mom. She tried to instill me with a little religion, but I'm afraid not much of it took. If most of the people I've met in my lifetime who believe they are going to heaven actually get there, I think I'll pass. It's not going to be a fun place. Anyway, just in case I'm mistaken, I think I've hedged my bets; I was baptized and confirmed a Lutheran, married in the Catholic church, and circumcised at a young age.

11

Poachers

There were hungry people in Cloquet as the Great Depression deepened. One family I knew went through a period when they had nothing to eat but oatmeal; they ate it as porridge for breakfast and fried at lunch and dinner. Mrs. Heikkila, who lived on Ninth Street, would comb through the boxcars parked on the railroad sidings near her home, searching out empty grain-hauling cars from which she swept up enough wheat residue to keep bread and flapjacks on her family's table. Community gardens were plotted out on vacant lots throughout town so people could try to grow a few vegetables. My father acquired a spot and planted potatoes. When the crop came up, it was smothered with beans. Some old-country Finn, unable to read signs written in English, had mistakenly planted his beans on top of our spuds. I don't remember that we ever realized any potatoes out of the effort.

My folks and I never went hungry although Dad was out of work for some time. Larson's Grocery, located behind Johnson Brothers' Hardware Store on South Tenth Street, carried us "on the book" until my father eventually got steady work at the paper mill. The final bill was over $900, a whopping figure when you consider that a modest home at the time could be purchased for $750 or less. It took my folks several years to pay off Larson's, but pay they did. Fortunately, carrying charges were practically unknown. No retail merchant would even propose such a thing. A man with a steady job could walk into Gamble's Lumber and Hardware, fill an order for enough material to build a complete home, agree verbally to pay so much a month on the account and never be asked for a penny of interest. (The local bank paid one-half of one percent on passbook savings.)

Our family's basic diet during this period centered around venison. We had an endless supply, because my father and his brother slipped easily from illegal moonshining to illegal jacklighting.

My father had constructed a garage behind our home on North Tenth Street. In winter, the unheated building was divided down the middle by a couple of huge tarpaulins hung from the rafters. On one side there was usually a car, either ours or one of Dad's brother's; on the other side, screened off by the tarps, were row upon row of hanging, frozen deer carcasses. It was like a storage locker in a meat-packing plant.

Private Nick Carlson (on left), U.S. Army, 1918.

Nick, one of my father's older brothers (they looked enough alike to be twins), came out of the army after World War I with psychiatric problems and a small disability pension. He was a quiet man who liked late-night poker games, often slept until noon, and played solitaire on his bed an hour or so each day. (He occupied one of the two upstairs bedrooms in our house on Tenth Street—the other was mine—and took his meals with us.) Underneath that calmness, however, was a very short fuse to a violent temper that exploded if he felt someone had perpetrated an injustice of some kind. I liked Nick a lot and was very saddened when he was taken away to spend the last third of his life behind the barbed wire-topped fences surrounding the criminally insane unit at the Minnesota State Hospital in St. Peter.

Supplying venison was Nick's forte. He, my father, and my uncle John who lived with some of the other Carlsons in shacks near the railroad tracks did most of their hunting at night. They carried a fully-charged car battery in a gunnysack to power a huge spotlight, Nick's pride and joy. When the brothers were out shining the fields long ahead of the sun, Nick would get a big chuckle out of directing the beam into some farmer's chicken coop. The resident rooster, thinking it was morning, would start sounding his wake-up call and rousing his cackling hens.

At first the brothers just hunted meat for personal use, but then John became friendly with the truck driver who delivered movie films twice a week to the Leb Theater across the street from our house. All winter long, the truck would return to the Twin Cities with a load of deer carcasses. Supposedly, they were delivered to some high-dollar "Sportsmen's Club" that daily offered venison on its menu. The poachers' cut of the money involved couldn't have been much, but every little bit helped in those hard times.

Poaching deer was fraught with risks. Game wardens and informers abounded. Once, hunting during daylight hours, John shot a deer and dragged it to a remote roadside where it had been pre-arranged that he'd be picked up by my uncle Swen in his Model A Ford. When John came out of the woods with the deer, there sat a man in a car whom John guessed was the law (game wardens didn't wear uniforms in those days). John looked the warden straight in the eyes and said, "I've got another one down back in the brush. Keep an eye on this one for me while I go get it and I'll cut you a share." The warden, probably figuring that two deer would make a better case than one, agreed. John reentered the woods never to return.

Sometimes the jacklighters seemed more interested in worrying the game wardens than they were in bagging meat. It became a contest, a sort of swamp tag.

One night my father, his brothers Nick and John, and a good friend of Dad's named Art Maunu were out spotting the fields for a shine of eyes when Art, who was driving, dropped one wheel of their Dodge into a ditch. Everybody except the driver was out of the car attempting to push it back onto the road when along came two game wardens in a Model A Ford. The wardens must have guessed they'd stumbled into a nest of poachers, but it was a lion-by-the-tail situation for them; the four men were big, and it was dark and lonely out there in the swamplands.

One of the wardens tried twice to look into the back seat of the Dodge with his flashlight, but Nick somehow managed to block his view each time. Finally, the man tittered nervously and asked, "You boys aren't carrying any guns are you?"

The foursome laughed and Art cracked something like, "What would we have guns for? We ain't got no pregnant daughters needing husbands!"

The two wardens helped shove the mired car back onto the road and continued on their way. Once they were settled into the Dodge, however, the poachers weren't long in overtaking the Ford. My father, sitting in the back seat, said, "Let's show them if we got guns!" As Art swung the Dodge around the slower moving Model A, Dad shoved the muzzle of his .32 caliber Winchester lever-action rifle out the window and, with fire blasting three feet out of the end of the barrel, pumped four quick rounds across the Ford's hood. Art, yee-hawing like a madman, stomped the gas pedal to the floor, leaving the wardens in a cloud of dust and flying gravel.

Nothing ever came out in the papers about the incident, and the law never showed up at our door. Either the wardens didn't know who they had tangled with, or they decided, for whatever reason, not to pursue the matter.

Very little venison was ever wasted. One exception was the time Hakey Aho joined the hunters. It was during legal hunting season, the annual fall stag party (if you'll forgive the pun) in Minnesota, and everyone was on good behavior and licensed.

Deer hunters, Frank (left) and Swen (right) Carlson (circa 1938).

The method of hunting in season was to drive the animals. Shooters would position themselves on "stands"—stumps, rocks, any high point—while the rest of the party fanned out and drove the deer toward them. Hakey didn't have a rifle but he had a bottle of whisky, most of it inside him, and he was content to beat the brush for the others. Doing his duty, he jumped a big buck. The deer, forced into the open and surrounded by shooters, many in the same happy condition as Hakey, was caught in heavy crossfire and went down almost immediately.

Hakey was the first to reach the animal. Out of breath and sweating profusely from his stagger through the windfalls and spongy muskeg, he plopped down on the buck's hindquarters, took a long pull on his bottle, and started to total up the bullet wounds on the carcass. He was poking his index finger into each hole as he counted in Finnish, "*Yksi* (one), *kaksi* (two), *kolme* (three), *neljä* (four), *viisi* (five)," when the buck suddenly leaped up, sending Hakey rolling as it disappeared into the surrounding woods.

My father, with the aid of our dog Midnight, searched on and off for nearly three weeks before he finally found the animal's remains. It had gone several miles before it died. The quest, of course, accomplished nothing. Dad just had to know.

The hobos who lived in the Hoover Camp down by the railroad tracks during the summer had our place flagged with a blaze cut into the telephone pole out front. Having no refrigeration, my mother canned venison in quart jars by the gross. Just about every other day one or two of the residents from the camp would turn up on our back steps (they never came to the front door and, after knocking at the back, would step down off the porch and wait on the walk). Mom would give them two quarts of meat for their "mulligan" with the stipulation that she wanted her jars back. She never lost one jar and they were always returned sparkling clean.

One of Cloquet's dentists, Doc Whittemore, had an office on Cloquet Avenue not far from our house. From time to time, he accepted gifts of venison from my uncle John in lieu of cash for dental work. Doc was a man who squeezed a nickel until both the Indian and the buffalo felt they'd been joined in wedlock. He would, to get his money's worth, chew Peerless tobacco until all the "good" had been extracted, place the totally masticated cud in the sun on the window sill in his office to dry, and then smoke it in an old, foul-smelling corncob pipe.

One fall, caught up in the annual hunting frenzy but too tight to buy a license, Doc Whittemore asked my uncle John to take him jacklighting. The two conspirators, well fortified against snake bites and other possible venoms, threw their light on an isolated hayfield where, to their surprise and joy, they spotted a young moose. With one lucky shot, Doc knocked the animal down. They were toasting their good fortune when John discovered that their "moose" had been to a farrier and fitted with iron shoes. The "moose" was a mule!

Doc was a penny-pincher, but he was also basically honest. The next day he returned to the scene and paid for the animal, throwing in a bit of free dental work to guarantee the farmer's silence.

I doubt that Doc ate the mule, but given his abhorrence of waste . . . ?

Although there were quite a number of Maunus scattered throughout the hinterlands of northern Minnesota, I was only acquainted with three of them. Wild men, they were tough Finns and full of jovial hell. They worked hard when employment was available, drank hard (my folks once took Andrew Maunu into our home and nursed him through the delirium tremens so he wouldn't have to go to the state hospital), and played hard.

I never knew Andrew all that well. He was, as I remember him, a tall man—six-foot three or better—with an angular build and a shy grin. He and my uncle Swen were good buddies, so I can only assume that he was at least peripherally involved in some of the Carlsons' illegal activities. If he wasn't directly implicated in the booze business, he was at least a good customer.

Andrew was a party animal and a ladies' man, a combination that ultimately played a small part in his death. Some years after the bootlegging/poaching era, Andrew, winding up a night of revelry, hired a taxi to take him to his home in Esko, Minnesota (Esko's Corner in those days). Arriving in Esko, the cab driver, intent on dropping his passenger at his door, made an illegal U-turn in the middle of the highway and was broadsided by another automobile. Andrew Maunu died instantly.

Ed Maunu operated a gasoline station and garage on Highway 61, Esko's main thoroughfare. I can only recall meeting him once, but he was a friend of my folks. I was eleven or twelve years old, and Mom and I had been to Duluth for a doctor's appointment. We were on our way back to Cloquet when our car's engine began to sputter, and huge clouds of blue smoke emitted from its exhaust system. We were approaching Esko, so Mom coaxed the vehicle into Ed's shop. Ed was on his back under another car as we pulled in and Mom called out, "Hey, Ed, my rear end's smoking. Can you take a look at it?"

Ed laughed until he was so weak he could hardly slide out from under the automobile. Working between fits of debilitating mirth, he finally got us on our way.

Art Maunu was the fighter of the threesome. Big and raw-boned, he loved to brawl just for the exercise. His idea of a fun Saturday night was to attend a country dance, consume a fair amount of white lightning, and wait for the inevitable free-for-all to commence. When the first punch was thrown, Art would put his broad back to a wall, laugh like a braying jackass, and dare all comers to take him. A lot of good men tried without success. Art would lay them out as fast as they came at him. My father told me that in one memorable fight at a gathering place named Sixty-Two Hall, Art piled up twelve unconscious challengers—his all-time high score.

Art and his wife, Hazel, were good friends of my parents. We'd often drive out to their small farm near Floodwood, Minnesota, just to visit. Their farm was a sub-subsistence operation of a few dairy animals and a lot of mud and cow dung squeezed in among the stumps left from the logging era. To make ends meet, Art drove trucks and snowplows for the county and, later, school bus for the school district.

Art loved anything with wheels and was an excellent, albeit sometimes creative, driver. I remember one evening when Art, Hazel, their three kids, my folks, and I were traveling on the back roads out of Floodwood in Art's 1933 or 1934 Studebaker. It was springtime and the whole countryside was inundated with snow melt and over-flowing creeks. The Studebaker was creeping along through water better than a foot deep while Art guessed the route by staying mid-way between the telephone poles lining both sides of the road. Wondering how deep we were running, Art, both hands on the steer-ing wheel, asked my father, who was sitting in the front seat next to him, to open his door and check the water level. The Studebaker's doors opened at their front edge, swinging out and to the rear. When Dad did as he was bid, the water, higher than expected, tore the door from his grip and a flood swept into the car. Drowning the interior of their automobile would upset most people, but not Art. He thought the whole episode was hilarious and roared with glee as we sat in cold water up to our backsides all the way to their farm.

Some of Art's antics frightened his wife half to death—like the time he went moose hunting using the Studebaker as his weapon. Late one night Art, Hazel, and their three kids were returning to their farm after visiting with friends when the Studebaker's headlights picked out a huge bull moose sauntering up the middle of the road ahead of them. Moose were extremely rare in the area, having been hunted to near extinction years earlier. Art decided this one had to be his. Gripping the steering wheel with both hands, whooping and yelling like a Saturday-matinee cattle rustler making off with the herd, Art bore down on the surprised moose. Instead of taking to the brush, the animal elected to race the car. Great clods of mud and gravel, flying off the bull's hoofs, shattered the Studebaker's wind-shield and one headlight as the engine roared, Art yee-hawed, and Hazel screamed, "Art, you damned fool, you're going to kill us all!"

The moose did his best but finally realized that he was no match for the machine and veered off into the woods. Art, stymied by a ditch, gave up the chase. Hazel, once she'd regained her composure, asked her husband, "Did you ever consider what you were going to do with the animal if you got him down? There's not a thing in this car you could have used to finish it off."

Art laughed, patted Hazel affectionately on the knee and answered, "Hell, Honey, you'd have talked him to death!"

Hazel passed away in middle age after suffering a massive stroke. Art never remarried and died of cancer in his early sixties.

12

More Folks

With the repeal of the Eighteenth Amendment and the simultaneous crunch of the Great Depression, our family's economic health deteriorated drastically. Unable to find other employment and refusing to go on welfare, my father and mother reluctantly went back to work at the Hotel Solem. They were paid a dollar a day which amounted to about six and one-half cents an hour.

We were poor, but nobody told me. Since all of our neighbors were also struggling to survive, there was no comparative scale to make me aware of the depths of our poverty. I know that all of the kids living on the three streets north of Cloquet Avenue spent considerable time gathering bits of coal scattered along the railroad tracks by passing trains and stashing it away for winter use. Sympathetic firemen stoking the huge steam-driven locomotives always threw a few shovelfuls of the black diamonds our way as they highballed down the line. Sometimes we speeded up our collecting by helping ourselves to "leaks" around loose boards in the railroad company's coal-storage sheds.

Unemployment, especially for men used to going to work and having a place to spend their days, can be very boring. And boredom often leads to mischief. Two brothers in their late twenties or early thirties living on lower Tenth Street were the owners of a limping Model T Ford for which they couldn't afford fuel. Situated next to the railroad tracks and across the street from their home were the Standard Oil Company's gasoline storage tanks. The brothers spent a lot of time sitting on the steps at the front of their house and watching the trains come and go, especially those that delivered the gasoline to Standard's tanks. One night, they tapped a spigot into one of the tank's drainage lines. Suddenly people began to notice that the old Model T never seemed to stay in one place, and the brothers and their friends were often off on fishing trips to far-flung parts of Minnesota. They were never charged with theft but were "asked" by the oil company's manager in the presence of the Chief of Police to cease and desist. The old Ford rarely moved again.

My grandfather, the old man, had a knack for shaking the neighborhood out of the doldrums. Forever puttering in his small blacksmith shop, he was experimenting with some kind of autoclave distilling apparatus when something went awry. (Prohibition was over, but he hoped it was a mistake that would soon be rectified. Maybe he was trying to produce a facsimile of Anchor Steam Beer. He never said.) As a rule, no one paid much attention to the old man's tinkering. This day, however, the quiet of the muggy, lazy summer's afternoon was suddenly shattered by an explosion of tremendous force. People, some of whom hadn't moved quickly in years, poured from their homes not knowing what to expect. Others, like my father, immediately converged on the shop. They found the old man standing mute and unscathed (he did complain for a while about a ringing in his ears), his blue eyes big and round behind his wire-rimmed glasses, staring up at the azure Minnesota sky through a six-foot-diameter hole in his roof. It was later estimated that the entire top of the riveted boiler section of his project had plowed the opening weighed in the neighborhood of two hundred pounds. Days of searching, however, yielded nothing of the missing hardware. Either the old man achieved orbital space capability twenty-five years ahead of Sputnik, or the wayward missile is at the bottom of the St. Louis River, a half mile from its launch site.

Another time, my grandfather decided to build an electric forge and eliminate the need to purchase coke. Considering the cost of a kilowatt-hour of electricity, the plan seemed ludicrous. However, the old man had no intention of enriching the Minnesota Power and Light Company; he bypassed the meter and, in the process, the fuses. The tranquility north of Cloquet Avenue was again treated to a bomb-like blast, a double whammy as the shock wave echoed from the hill north of the river. The copper coil in the new forge had turned white hot when the overload blew a transformer clean off a lightpole down the street. By the time employees of the power company appeared, the old man had removed his meter-jumper and was righteously complaining about his lack of electric light due to their equipment failures.

One day in the spring of 1935, my father came through the back doorway into our house on Tenth Street walking on air. He'd been hired by the Balsam Wool Company (later the Wood Conversion Company and now the CONWED Corporation) for the going wage of 34.5 cents an hour! President Hoover's belated prosperity had finally rounded our corner, and both Mom and Dad bailed out of the Hotel Solem.

The new job lasted six weeks when, without fanfare, the company decided to eliminate some of its payroll. Lacking seniority, Dad couldn't survive the cut. Desperate, my father went to the Weyerhaeuser Paper Mill, informed the official in charge of the time office that he was going to stay there until they hired him and took a seat on a bench just outside the door. Realizing that he meant it, they put him to work clearing brush from under some power lines. When that job was finished, he worked wherever and whenever they needed an extra man until the millwright boss discovered Dad was good with tools. They put him on a mill maintenance crew—a steady job, a regular pay check, and the opportunity to learn the millwright trade, which he followed until his retirement many years later.

Quite a number of the female teachers working in the Cloquet schools resided at the Hotel Solem; housing for single women who wanted to escape some of the small-town scrutiny educators were subjected to just didn't exist anywhere else in the community. Neither Hans nor Lucy objected to discreet partying or carnal intemperance, so the hotel became an oasis for fun-loving ladies of the teaching profession who were otherwise expected to be chaste and eternally sober.

Very few of my schoolmates realized that their teachers, prim and proper all week long, behaved much like human beings on Friday and Saturday nights, but I did. I knew, because they threw their empty whisky bottles out of the hotel's upper-story windows into our yard. At least they did until one winter's night when some inebriate opened her window and, forgetting there was also a storm window, gave the empty a fling. Glass cost money, and the Solems put a quick end to the practice.

I once overheard a traveling tombstone salesman tell my father, "A stop at the Hotel Solem is like free samples night in a whorehouse." (I thought the man said, "horror house." It was quite a while before I finally got my "horrors" sorted out.)

Anyone who was around during World War II will remember the KILROY WAS HERE graffiti. It spread across at least six of the seven continents (Antarctica may have been an exception). Well, Cloquet had its own Kilroy type in the early 1930s. His name was Kaka Peters.

Kaka's given name was Frederick although I doubt even he knew that until he registered for the draft and went into the U.S. Army. He was a teen-ager who claimed four choice possessions: a yellow and tan shepherd-mongrel named Fido, an unlimited supply of nondescript paints scrounged from "empty" cans behind Tony's Auto Paint Shop on Tenth Street, a brush (aerosol wasn't yet available), and the walkingest shoes in northern Minnesota. He must have also harbored an unconscious, consuming desire for immortality because no matter where one traveled a hundred miles in any direction from Cloquet, walls, rocks, railroad overpasses, and bridge abutments, all proclaimed in large block characters KAKA & FIDO. I once read a letter to the editor in *The Duluth Herald* from some perplexed reader in the Twin Cities who wanted to know what the KAKA & FIDO plastered all over our part of the state meant. The editor didn't know, but everyone in the bailiwick north of Cloquet Avenue did.

Kaka, a colloquialism, possibly of Scandinavian origin, means shit. It's hard to imagine a youngster going through life so designated, but he did, and we thought nothing of it. I would think the inherent psychological ramifications on the individual would provide enough material for at least two doctoral theses.

Both Kaka and Fido are gone now. The last time I was in Minnesota, I kept a sharp eye out for one of the old signs. Surely, I thought, one must have escaped the sand-blasters and painter-overers. But I never found one.

My father used to say, "When Ida closes one eye, it's 'feet do your duty' time!" The eldest of the fourteen Carlson children, Ida, was the "mama's girl" of the family. Whereas her brothers and sisters couldn't leave the nest fast enough, she was content to remain close to her mother's skirts.

The old man, however, figured the senior daughter should logically be the first to leave the fold. When a twenty-seven-year-old man named Louis Newman hitched up a team of horses and journeyed all the way to Moose Lake from Cloquet to ask for another daughter's hand, my grandfather, a shrewd horse trader's glint in his eye, suggested, "Why don't you take Ida instead?"

Newman binked twice and insisted that he wanted her sixteen-year-old sister Olga.

After some continued negotiation, the old man could see that the suitor's mind was made up and gave him begrudging permission to marry the girl of his choice.

Ida, not a pretty girl and virtually hidden from the world in the sparsely populated backwoods (Olga had preceded Lucy to Cloquet where she met Newman), had small opportunity for meeting males intent on marriage. The old man had about decided his first-born was going to be an albatross around his neck forever when, at about age twenty, she became pregnant. A man named Otto Lehto owned up to the deed and married Ida. Eight months after their son Eddie was born, however, Lehto suffered a nervous breakdown and was committed to the Minnesota State Hospital in Fergus Falls. Ida soon took up with a cheerful Finn named Henry Aho.

Henry and Ida didn't marry for some years because they had been told the law wouldn't allow her to divorce her husband while he was a patient in a mental hospital. That, of course, didn't still the pri-mordial urgings, and Ida had three more children before she and Henry finally married in 1924.

(Ida's firstborn, Eddie Lehto, took Henry's last name as his own, but the two never got along. As a young man, Eddie began shipping on the Great Lakes, moving to salt water sailoring with the advent of World War II. Never legally adopted by Henry, he went back to being a Lehto to ease the paperwork involved in acquiring his Merchant Marine certificates. After the war, Eddie lived off and on on San Francisco's skid row and finally just disappeared. His sisters tried several times to locate him without success, but they came away fairly convinced that their brother was in all probability one of the many unidentified victims of mass murderer Juan V. Corona who made a career of recruiting crop laborers and burying them along the Sacramento River in California. One of the sisters, however, couldn't let it rest. She kept nagging the authorities—missing persons' bureaus, the seamen's unions, government agencies—until, finally, in 1988 she learned through the Social Security Administration that her brother had died a derelict in Portland, Oregon, on October 18, 1978, at age sixty-five.

Once the Social Security people passed on the information as to which funeral home in Portland had taken care of Eddie's remains, his sister contacted me. Living close to Portland, I finally located his remains in a cemetery vault along with nearly a hundred other unclaimed boxes of ashes. The undertaker who opened the vault warned me that it might be impossible to find Eddie's container in the pile; roofs of mausoleums sometimes leak (the inhabitants never complain) and labels soak off and are lost. He nearly had a fit when I said any box would do and that I'd never tell, informing me he would never be party to such a deception. We did, after a short search, find a box properly identified as Eddie's, so I never had a chance to really test the man's resolve.

The undertaker wanted thirty-five dollars, on top of his sizeable fee to open the vault, to ship Eddie's ashes to Cloquet. (I mailed them parcel post for $2.95.)

Henry Aho was a happy, carefree drunk who worked from time to time in the mills around Cloquet. He was known variously as "Hakey," "Three-Day Henry" (three days' work and he'd go on a binge until the money ran out), and "Boom-Boom" (the result of his expertise with dynamite on construction projects around the Northwest Paper Company's Mill). With the repeal of Prohibition, Henry became a regular at Marv O'Hearn's tavern on Cloquet Avenue, and Ida became a termagent devoted to berating the man for his erring ways. When Henry would stagger home from O'Hearn's, Ida would close one eye and let fly with whatever was handy. Once, I happened on the scene just as Henry, on a dead run, burst from their shack two steps ahead of airborne tableware and the drawer from the kitchen table. Another time, in the middle of winter, it was the full ash pan from their wood stove, hot ashes streaming behind like spent fuel from a ballistic missile.

Not that Henry needed much urging, Ida's constant haranguing did little except to drive him even further into the bottle. Henry's other solaces were a tame crow and Midnight, a faithful old black dog with one flopped ear. The three would trudge up Tenth Street past our house most every morning on their daily trip to O'Hearn's— Henry with Midnight at his heels and the crow perched on the dog's back. If Henry was without funds, he'd stop at our place and borrow a quarter "for an eye opener." Somehow, he always managed to pay it back the next day.

Henry and the crow would enter the tavern and share the five schooners of brew a quarter would buy (Henry and the crow alternated sips from each mug) while Midnight waited patiently on the sidewalk outside. When they came out, Henry would have a good start on the day, and the crow would be smashed out of his black head. The threesome would trudge back down the hill, Henry fortified to face Ida's tirades and the crow on the peck for Caliber, Aho's orange tabby. (When the cat was young, he jumped onto my uncle Oscar's lap and, as cats are prone to do, tail up, turned his backside to Oscar's face. Oscar squinted and said, "That's about .30 caliber!" And Caliber the cat was named.)

It was Ida's constant carping about her husband's sodden ways that triggered the incident that put my uncle Nick away for life.

My father always maintained that Nick's mental problems were caused by army negligence. Dad guessed that his brother's condition resulted from too many innoculations brought about by a snafu in military record keeping or perhaps even medical experimentation with untried influenza vaccines. He may have been right. After Nick was drafted, he was sent to Camp Forest, Georgia, where, according to Veterans Administration records, he came down with a case of the deadly, worldwide 1918 influenza that lasted eleven days. From Georgia, he was transferred to Fort Dodge, Iowa, and honorably discharged in accordance with War Department demobilization orders at the end of World War I. His physical examination on discharge supposedly revealed no medical problems.

Nick was living with his brother Alex and Shotgun Hilda in Superior, Wisconsin, when he started having mental problems—mood swings, temper tantrums. On February 25, 1922, Shotgun Hilda managed to have Nick committed to the Veterans Psychiatric Hospital in Mendota, Wisconsin. He was there eighteen months, out for three weeks, and back again for four more months. Diagnosed as suffering from service-connected dementia praecox—simple type, he was granted a total disability pension of seventy-five dollars per month. True, psychiatry was in its infancy, but I find it difficult to understand how dementia praecox could be service connected when Nick served less than three months. Given our government's and our military's propensity for hiding the truth, it makes my father's supposition at least possible.

Released from the hospital, Nick moved to Cloquet where his psychosis apparently deepened over the years. Eventually, it was decided that he couldn't be trusted to handle his pension, and Hans Solem somehow had the hotel's bookkeeper appointed guardian to manage it (later, Hans' eldest daughter took over the job).

Nick never caused any serious problems when he lived with us on Tenth Street. He stayed busy helping my father rebuild our house and going on nighttime forays in search of deer. He seemed mostly content. The few times he did throw temper tantrums because of some real or imagined offense, my mother would quietly tell him to behave and go to his room until he cooled off, and he would.

(My mother had a real knack for handling crazies. Once when my uncle John was in the throes of delirium tremens, he went into Johnson Brothers' Department Store on Cloquet Avenue and proceeded to try on all the shoes in stock. Reynold Johnson, one of the store's owners and a knowing man, played along with the situation until John decided that he needed to remove the heels from all of the shoes to "get the numbers printed underneath them." At that point, Mr. Johnson panicked and sent a clerk running to fetch my mother. Mom went to the store, quietly told John it was time to leave, and he followed her home like a well-behaved child. He was sent to the Moose Lake State Hospital to dry out.)

In October 1939, Nick offered to help his sister Ida's husband, Henry Aho, replace the rotting footings under their shack. The two men were hardly started when Henry went on a bender and began spending his days in O'Hearn's tavern instead of working on the home repair. This, of course, didn't sit well with Nick, who was not a drinker. Even so, all might have been resolved without incident except for Ida's loud, incessant complaining. With Henry out of earshot in the tavern, she focused her lamentations on her brother, much like a preacher carping at those in church about the sinners who didn't show, until the tenuous line between peace and rage in Nick's mind snapped.

Nick was working with a pickax under the house and took it with him as he stormed up the street toward O'Hearn's. The bartender saw him as he crossed Cloquet Avenue on a beeline for the tavern. With the aid of a number of his customers, the bartender wrestled the weapon away from Nick and held him down until the police arrived.

Nick maintained he never intended to do Henry bodily harm, only to frighten him enough to stop his drinking. The court didn't buy it. Nick was adjudged criminally insane and sent to the St. Peter State Hospital. According to hospital records, he worked in the kitchen and never required any special treatment or tranquilizing drugs.

In 1954, my wife and I visited Nick at St. Peter. I hadn't seen him in nearly twenty years, yet, except for normal aging, he looked much the same as I remembered him. We visited across the table, my wife and I on one side and Nick on the other flanked by two husky orderlies. He didn't know me until I told him I was "Frankie-*poika*" (Finn for "Frank's boy"). He asked how my folks were, what my father was doing for a living, and if I'd seen any of his other brothers (he never mentioned either Ida or Henry). I asked him if he needed anything—cigarettes, candy. He said no, he'd quit smoking and had everything he needed. Then, he asked me if he was in the county jail. Surprised, I answered no, a hospital. He just laughed; I could see the barred doors and windows, too.

On September 19, 1957, Nick was released from St. Peter State Hospital and transported by ambulance to St. Mary's Hospital in Duluth where he died of cancer of the colon October 4, 1957, age sixty. He had spent seventeen years and eleven months in the cages of St. Peter's unit for the criminally insane.

Twenty-eight years after Nick's death, I was going through his file from St. Peter State Hospital and found a copy of a letter to the superintendent from a Veterans Administration lawyer. It was dated February 18, 1955. The attorney wanted to know if it would be all right for Nick to purchase a television set. Nick wanted one for the hospital kitchen where he worked and felt it would be a good use for some of his accumulated pension funds. The file doesn't say if Nick's request was granted. I suppose I could find out, but I don't really want to know. . . . I'd like to believe that a man allotted so little in life got at least one small thing he wanted.

13

Tough Men and Hardy Women

Almost without exception, my father, Frank, and his eight brothers were brawlers. They reveled in it. Growing up with the constant need to do battle to hold their places in the large family pecking order probably had a lot to do with their combative natures. "Don't tread on me!" would have been the motto on their coat of arms had they possessed one.

In his prime, Swen was probably the toughest scraper of the bunch. Six feet, three inches of compact muscle and bone, he was a man to be reckoned with. Growing up in the mining community of Crosby, Minnesota, he fought in a few smokers and considered pursuing a boxing career. With no one to guide him, however, the dream died.

My father could also bang with the best of them, and it didn't take much provocation to get him started. The sun coming up on the Fourth of July was excuse enough.

Cloquet's annual Independence Day celebration began officially with a parade down Cloquet Avenue. The procession was typical of those held all across small-town America: the high school band, an American Legion contingent, a fire truck, a few politicians wearing stiff, white straw hats with red and blue hatbands, and a spattering of service club members riding their respective floats, all proudly led by my friend Willard's father, Carl Bodin. Mr. Bodin—ramrod straight, well embalmed and fortified by ten A.M., resplendent in his World War I army uniform complete with wrapped leggings and overseas cap—carried the American flag, his jaundiced eyes focused glassily on the avenue's center line, which eventually reeled him and his trailing entourage into Pinehurst Park and disbandment.

Once the parade was over, Pinehurst became the focal point of Cloquet's collective celebration. Carnival rides, championship birling contests, baseball games, political speeches, and food stands offering hamburgers and hot dogs with plenty of cold beer and soda pop to wash it all down. The festivities culminated in the evening with a fireworks display and accompanying "oohs" and "ahhs."

Normally, my father was not a fighting drunk. Alcohol made him want to sing and dance and have a good time. For some reason, though, the July heat coupled with cold beer would set him off. I think he managed at least one battle every Fourth of July during those years we lived on Tenth Street. They often had their roots in some past incident from the bootlegging days or some unresolved Saturday night altercation at a country dance, and they invariably ended quickly with Dad's adversary sitting dumbly on his buns trying not to swallow dislodged teeth.

Dad's last Fourth of July rampage, when I was about ten years old, was his most memorable. It started over a dill pickle. Mom, Dad, and I were sitting at the counter of one of the hamburger stands in Pinehurst Park when a stool pigeon from Prohibition days walked behind my father, reached across his shoulder and plate, and snatched a pickle from a condiment dish. The fink was purposely trying to annoy my father and probably felt secure, because two policemen were at that moment passing by. His feeling was short lived. He was still clutching the pickle when his butt hit the ground. He scrambled back to his feet (a bad mistake), struck a classic John L. Sullivan pose, and was flattened by an uppercut he never saw. The two policemen, with help from some bystanders, grabbed my father and walked him off in one direction while his antagonist was hauled away by the armpits in the other, his heels dragging two furrows in the dust.

Once the combatants were separated, the police released my father with the suggestion there be no more fisticuffs. There wasn't . . . for a while. Later in the day, with the temperature rising and the cold beer flowing, Dad crossed paths with his first victim's brother. My father always claimed that the man came looking for him. At any rate, with a few trusted seconds in attendance, they retired to a wooded area of the park. I wasn't present but have it on good authority that Dad eliminated a considerable amount of future dental hygiene chores for the challenger.

We stayed around for the fireworks, which closed the festivities, and started the walk home. Dad must have taken on something stronger than beer by this time. Whatever it was, mixed with his pumped up adrenalin, it was explosive. We were moving east on Cloquet Avenue in the vicinity of the public library when we met two men going in the opposite direction. For no reason I could understand, my father leveled his sights on the larger of the pair and lowered the boom, leaving the hapless man sitting on the sidewalk holding his jaw and exclaiming, "God . . . damn!" The downed victim stayed where he was while his friend backed off and said nothing.

Mom grabbed my father by the arm and steered him up the sidewalk toward home as she gave him verbal hell, but he wasn't listening. Reaching the Texaco gasoline station on the corner of Eighth Street and Cloquet Avenue, Dad took a swing at a heavy metal Texaco sign, sending it flying into the street. The act would have broken an average man's hand, but it didn't seem to phase him.

My father must have been about thirty-five or thirty-six years old at the time, an advanced age for a brawler, and that Fourth of July was sort of his peak. A steady job at the paper mill, regular hours, and, no doubt, a few uncompromising ultimatums from my mother tended to mellow him somewhat. He never backed away from a fight in his life, but he quit actively seeking them after that triple-header day.

My dad's brother Oscar was a man of great physical strength. Years after his death, I met a fellow who had worked with Oscar for a time at the match factory (also known as the toothpick factory) in Cloquet. It seems they were stacking heavy crates of some kind, and Oscar was throwing them up to the workers high atop the piles. My informant said, "When Oscar tossed those crates, you never tried to catch one on its way up. If you did, you went with it. We'd let them go by and catch them on their way down."

I was too young to remember which house we were living in at the time, but I recall getting up one morning and finding a foot-square hole in the kitchen wall. When I asked about it, my mother said that my uncle John had been sitting there the evening before when, in the heat of a disagreement of some kind, Oscar took a swing at him. John ducked, and Oscar's fist continued on like an armor-piercing missile. This wasn't the communion wafer-strength plaster-board construction so common today; this wall was tongue-and-groove lumber covered with heavy felt and wallpaper. As far as I know, Oscar didn't break his hand.

In keeping with family tradition, my father insisted that I fight my own battles. The first winter that we lived in the house directly behind the Hotel Solem, I managed to run afoul with a couple of bigger kids who vowed to wreak havoc on my body. They chased me home from school and waited ominously across the street for me to come out. I sniffled and cried, expecting dear old Dad to come to my rescue. He didn't. Instead, he ordered, "Go back out and fight them!"

"They're bigger than me," I wailed, "and there's two of them!" He wouldn't listen. Taking my arm, he shoved me out the door, shutting it behind me. I took one look at the waiting assassination squad and went right back inside.

"I can't fight two of them!" I howled.

"Then even the odds!" With that, Dad took a stick of firewood from the box near the kitchen rage, handed it to me, and pushed me back outside.

The incident taught me two things that have served me well in life: (1) It's possible to even the odds in almost every situation, and (2) There's usually room for negotiation. I put down the stick, walked across the street and ironed out our differences with some damned fast oratory. Dad never asked how I solved my problem, but I'm sure he watched the whole thing from our living room window.

As do most kids, I had a few fights that couldn't be avoided, but I never enjoyed the pain involved and side-stepped physical violence whenever possible. I'd seen enough of the aftermaths of some of my father's and his brothers' battles and couldn't fathom the delights of black eyes and broken teeth. Maybe I have a little of the old man in me; long, long before the hippie generation, I decided that making love far surpasses making war.

The five girls in the Carlson family were also fighters in their own way. Lucy was like Johnny Cash's "Sue." She enjoyed getting right down in the broken glass, blood, and beer and mixing it with the boys. Her love of booze and her constant quest for what she called "the high life" usually put her where the action was, and she had the physical strength to hold her own. In retrospect, I would guess that brawling gave her a release for pent up energy. She was prone to complain loudly and bitterly to everyone that Hans Solem was no good in bed, an observation I find hard to comprehend considering his overall track record.

I never knew my aunt Olga very well. She and her husband Louis Newman left Cloquet right after the Great Fire and opened a bar in Menomonie, Wisconsin. The bar was ostensibly converted to a confectionery during Prohibition—at least that's what the sign on the window said. Old snapshots of Olga and Louis lined up in front of the place with some of their customers show happy faces not usually associated with milk shake consumption. Of course, the business quickly reverted to a bar again when the country came back to its senses.

Newman was probably a good man early in his marriage to Olga, but he suffered a series of disabling strokes after they moved to Menomonie and spent many years confined to a wheelchair. Olga ran the tavern, took care of Louis, raised one daughter of her own and one of her sister Ida's sons pretty much by herself for years.

Eleven years younger than her disabled husband, Olga naturally had needs that Louis couldn't possibly supply in his physical condition. I don't know if Olga played around in Menomonie, but when she visited Cloquet, which she did about once a year, she pulled out all the stops. While Hans Solem sat on his leather throne in the hotel's lobby, chewing his cigars and savoring his self-importance, Lucy and Olga would party and play musical beds with the boys four stories above him and out of earshot. I must have been about seven years old when, hanging around the hotel's basement, I chanced to overhear my two aunts comparing notes after one of their frolics. At the time, I really didn't understand what was being discussed, but they were rating men as having good, fair, or poor "bones." They weren't, I realized several years later, discussing skeletal structure.

I last saw Olga in 1954. My wife and I were passing through Wisconsin and stopped at the tavern in Menomonie. It was mid-morning and Olga had just opened for business. She was straightening up the place from the night before as we took seats at the bar. I ordered a good Wisconsin beer and watched her for a few minutes. Her hair was dyed bright red and her face was well hidden under heavy pancake makeup, but it was her hands that really caught my attention; the knuckles of her fingers were massively swollen with arthritis. She had to have been in a lot of pain. I let her know who I was, she brought me a second beer, and my wife and I went on our way.

Like all of us, Olga had her frailties, but she worked hard, she took care of her own, and she gave far more to others than she ever received in return. She died in a nursing home in Rhinelander, Wisconsin, June 13, 1968, at age seventy-six. Her only daughter, Charlotte, passed away a short time later. Char was terminally ill with cancer when Olga died but never told her mother. She didn't want to burden Olga with a problem she couldn't solve.

As far as I know, my aunt Ida was never involved in the revelry that spiced up the Hotel Solem. She did operate a blind pig and went to jail for it, but she really didn't have much choice. Henry "Hakey" Aho, her husband, was a drunkard who didn't provide for his family, so Ida was left to feed her children any way she could. With her brothers running booze and operating stills, one thing just led to another.

When Ida was incarcerated, her kids were farmed out to relatives on her husband's side of the family except for her youngest son who went to live with Olga in Menomonie; he eventually elected to stay there rather than return to Cloquet. Ida was in jail for several months. She was finally released when Lucy convinced the judge that justice was not being served by keeping the family separated. The judge actually visited the Aho home (purchased originally for $150) on lower Tenth Street to check it out for himself. He commented that he "didn't see how anyone could raise a family in those conditions" when he set her free. Somehow, under "those conditions," Ida raised her family and did a respectable job of it. Her children grew up to be productive, law-abiding citizens (and that includes her first son, Eddie. He may not have been a success by most of society's standards, but he apparently made his own way up to the time of his death).

Ida died in a nursing home in Carlton, Minnesota, March 10, 1971, age eighty-three.

My grandmother, Marjana Karlson, gave birth to her fourteenth and last baby on November 29, 1909. Two months later, her number two child, Hilda, brought home a newborn infant girl and dumped it on my grandmother to raise. Hilda never said who the father was. According to one of her sisters, Hilda was the archetype of the young, unwed mother who claimed not to know who the father of her child might be and explained it this way: "It was dark when he came to my bed and dark when he left, but he smelled like a shoemaker." There were several theories circulated through the family about Hilda's first pregnancy, none of them mentioning any bright stars in the East.

Hilda was one of those girls who seemed to get pregnant just thinking about it. She evidently thought about it a lot. She lived with one man long enough to have three more babies, married him while carrying his third, and then divorced him. She gave all four of her kids his name although she didn't even know him when the first one was born. A fifth baby, a girl, came on the scene later and was given up for adoption. She was last known to reside somewhere in California.

When Hilda's husband left her bed, or she his, she managed to raise the three children on welfare handouts, sporadic work at the

Hotel Solem, and, I suspect, some help from Lucy. With her insatiable need of men and blessed by the gods of fertility, Hilda had many pregnancies. Lucy, fortunately or unfortunately, depending on your view, seemed to know every curette artist in two states and solved Hilda's repeated dilemmas. I once asked one of my aunts how many abortions she guessed Hilda had had. The aunt raised her eyes to the heavens and answered, "Birds fly, fish swim, Hilda screws. Who knows?"

Hilda was well past middle age when she moved in with an extremely intemperate Pole by the name of Frank Gallus. My aunt Alena, something of a Puritan compared to her sisters, suggested it would be a good thing if they married, and she must have caught Mr. Gallus at a weak moment. Anyway, he let Alena make all the arrangements, and he showed up for the wedding with more sheets to the wind than a Cape Horn square-rigger. In the middle of the ceremony all the booze settled into his bladder. Frank told the minister to speed it up, and he and Hilda were married in record time. Instead of kissing the blushing bride, the groom hot-footed it to the men's room.

The wedding was a private affair, but the shivaree wasn't. Bozo Erickson and I attended carrying a thirty-six-inch circular saw blade between us on a stick. Armed with two hammers and alternating beats on the steel blade like a pair of drummers setting the rowing tempo for a crew of galley slaves, we not only shook the newlyweds out of bed, we drowned out the pot and pan bangers and caused possible hearing losses throughout the entire neighborhood. The bridegroom finally appeared and bought us off at ten cents a head, a price of a huge double-dip ice cream cone at the Dairy Inn on Cloquet Avenue.

Hilda's and Frank's marriage was a foot race from the start; he ran for the bars, and she tried to head him off before the rent money disappeared. Once, in an attempt to elude his wife on a cold, snowy winter's day, Frank shoved all of Hilda's shoes into their wood stove's roaring fire box and took off on foot through the drifts for town. She called a cab and was waiting in her stocking feet at his favorite watering hole when he arrived. They compromised—she got new shoes, and he got to wet his whistle.

Somehow, Hilda and Frank Gallus put up with each other, and both managed to live past the allotted three score and ten. Hilda died of natural causes April 27, 1965, at age seventy-four. Frank held on a couple of years longer. My aunt Alena, who lived in the adjacent house, would check on him from time to time. One morning she couldn't raise him when she pounded on his door. Entering, she found his body under his bed where he'd probably crawled in a futile attempt to escape the demons of delirium tremens.

In many ways Alena, the eleventh of the fourteen Carlson children, was the straight arrow of the bunch. Being the baby girl of the family and much younger than her sisters, they tended to shelter her rather than lead her astray. Like some of the others, she did go to work for Lucy at the Hotel Solem. She and my mother were about the same age and started working at the hotel in 1920 at ages sixteen.

Alena met her first husband, John Becklund, at a wiener roast. She didn't have an escort, and he was a handsome soldier home on leave. She wrote him a note inviting him to accompany her. He wrote back, "I'll be there with bells on." One thing led to another, and they eventually married.

John Becklund was a buck sergeant in the U.S. Army with fifteen years service behind him. Regarding his marriage, however, he decided that the post-World War I military didn't offer the wherewithal required to support a family, so he mustered out. A short while later, the Great Depression began, and he became a member of the army of the unemployed.

As a child, I thought John Becklund was a great guy. He had tattoos on his forearms, rolled his own cigarettes so that they looked almost tailor-made, and didn't seem to mind taking time to talk with the kids of the neighborhood. He regaled Bozo Erickson and me with wild tales of his army life in the Philippines. He was, however, not popular with his brothers and sisters-in-law. Like a lot of old soldier types, he probably tended to exaggerate some of his experiences. The collective Carlsons pegged him, rightly or wrongly, as a hot-air artist. Also, John Becklund had served as a prison guard at the U.S. Disciplinary Barracks, Fort Leavenworth, Kansas, during part of his military career, which made any family allegiance he might profess highly suspect.

Alena and John had tough going like most everybody during the Depression years, but they hung on. With the approach of World War II, hard times eased and John found steady work in a steel mill in Duluth, Minnesota. The job was hard, and John Becklund was no kid anymore. After twenty-seven years of marriage, he dropped dead of a heart attack.

Eventually, Alena met and married Emil Marsyla, a big, happy Finn. Emil and Alena enjoyed twenty-five years together before he succumbed to cancer at age eighty.

Alena, in her mid-eighties now, lives in a nursing home near her daughter in southern Minnesota.

In 1934 or 1935, the house next to ours on North Tenth Street was occupied by an elderly Finn named Matt Alaspa and his wife. Mrs. Alaspa was a huge woman who suffered a disability of some kind that kept her on crutches. Because of her great size and her infirmity, she never left the house.

On her death, it was discovered that Mrs. Alaspa had far too much corpulence for a regular casket, so the undertaker special-ordered one custom built for her at, of course, a greater cost. Unfortunately, however, no one thought to inform the gravedigger.

The pallbearers sweated and strained moving the lady's bulk from home to hearse, hearse to church, church back to hearse, hearse to gravesite, giving the minister ample opportunity to flaunt his eruditeness in front of the captive audience as was the practice of the times. Once at the cemetery, however, it was discovered that Mrs. Alaspa, resting in her customized box, was too wide for the waiting hole. It was a hot day, the burden had been great, patiences were worn thin. Anxious to be done with it, Matt Alaspa ordered, "Drop her in sideways!"

The Finnish-Lutheran minister nearly had apoplexy. He didn't know what Biblical law said a body had to be buried on its back, but he was certain there was one. He absolutely refused to even consider the proffered solution to the problem.

The funeral entourage stood sweltering in the hot sun while the gravedigger was summoned and the hole widened (at extra cost) so the lady could at last be laid to rest.

A few days after the funeral, my father was visiting with Mr. Alaspa across the fence separating their properties. In the course of the conversation the widower announced that he had placed an ad in the Finnish language newspapers for a new wife. "A skinny one," he confided, a crafty gleam in his eyes. "Cheaper!"

14

Family Skeletons

Besides my uncle Nick, my uncle Charley was the only other state-certi-
fied psychologically impaired member of the Carlson family. Born April
18, 1903, Charley purportedly suffered from "mental deficiency" all of
his life. The general family consensus was "he could never learn."

My personal memories of Charley are very vague. I just barely
remember him being around the Hotel Solem when we first moved to
Tenth Street. I do, however, distinctly recall visiting him at the Moose
Lake State Hospital, a few short miles from his birthplace, several years
later. He was a much thinner man than any of his brothers, and he gave
the impression of being very shy and ill at ease around others.

Charley was diagnosed as suffering from dementia praecox,
hebephrenic type. He was sixteen years old when he finally checked
out of the third grade in school, but he was definitely not as stupid as
the system and his family seemed to think. Reading his case history
years after his death left me with the belief that the ravages of typhoid
fever at age seven exacerbated by a lifetime without concerned care
probably destroyed what could have been a fulfilled existence.

When he was just a youngster, his father, the old man, taught
Charley to play the organ in the country church near Moose Lake.
Charley never learned to read music, but he could watch and listen
while someone else played and then step right in with a repeat performance. As a young man, before his first incarceration, he would
often go to the Leb Theater in Cloquet, watch the pianist in the
orchestra pit do his pre-movie stint and return to the Hotel Solem to
duplicate the performance on the Solems' piano.

In spite of his meager education, Charley had a real talent for
writing. It was common in those days for companies peddling salves,
ointments, seeds, and a gamut of snake oils to advertise for young
would-be Horatio Alger rags-to-riches hopefuls to be their sales rep-

resentatives. The companies, mail order outfits hustling to make a buck during the wheeling and dealing Twenties, ran glowing ads promising sure-fire success and wealth in all the pulp magazines. Charley would answer the ads and receive boxes of the products to sell. Some of the stuff he used, some he gave away, and if he did manage to make a sale, he spent the proceeds, all of it, on himself.

Naturally, threatening duns weren't long in coming, but they never fazed Charley. He would sit down and with beautiful penmanship inform his creditors that they were invading his privacy, that their products were not worth the expense of return postage, and if they did not cease their harassment, he would see them in court. Charley let my father read some of his replies to the demands for payments, and Dad was amazed. Years later he told me, "You'd have thought Clarence Darrow wrote them." One blast from Charley and the commissars of commerce never pressed him again. Charley's writing ability was apparently like his skill with music—a gift.

The Solems considered Charley to be something of an embarrassment, but he was basically free labor and they had no qualms about using him. They put him to work in the hotel laundry, buried away in the basement. Charley labored hard and received wages, but Lucy, as his guardian, handled his money. Like the coal miners of Appalachia before John L. Lewis, he was always in debt to the company store.

Charley, of course, did create some problems for the Solems. The hotel had large bins of keeper vegetables in the basement: rutabagas, turnips, potatoes, and the like. Charley, a true night person, would roam the hotel in the late hours. I suppose he was often bored by the lack of activity and companionship. One night, looking for something to do, he began throwing turnips against the back wall of their bin. Perhaps he was pretending to pitch baseball. As each turnip hit, a loud KA-THUMP echoed through the hotel, a wooden structure with a facing of brick and the reverberative qualities of a bass drum. The Solem residence on the first floor received the brunt of the impact. Jarred from his sleep, Hans Solem clad in a nightshirt extending to below his knees, his feet trying to find purchase in a pair of floppy slippers, hurried to the basement. He found nothing and returned to his bed. His head had no sooner hit the pillow when KA-THUMP, KA-THUMP, the strange sound returned.

The little game continued for several nights. Finally, some of the hotel's guests began to complain, so Lucy joined the search. It turned out that Charley, thin as he was, could inch his way around the supporting timbers in the basement and stay out of Hans' myopic, one-eyed vision no matter how diligently the man searched. (Lucy maintained that Hans, on retiring each night, put his "good" eye in a glass of water along with his teeth.) Once Lucy got into the act, Charley was trapped.

As he grew older, Charley's nocturnal wanderings took him farther and farther out into the community. Some citizens became uneasy about the gaunt, scarecrow-like wraith moving furtively about in the shadows at night, and Charley was committed to the state hospital in Fergus Falls, Minnesota, on February 6, 1925. He was twenty-one years old.

They let Charley out on September 13, 1928, into the custody of his sister Lucy. He was recommitted May 11, 1931, because, the official record states, "He gets angry easily, actions are those of a six- or eight-year-old child: throws rocks and sticks into the street. He has shown a disposition to injure others. He had typhoid fever at seven years of age." (I wonder how many of us supposedly sane individuals wouldn't be "disposed to injure others" if we were teased and ridiculed every time we did something foolish. As for "throwing rocks and sticks into the street," Tenth Street had a gravel surface, gravel is made up of rocks, Charley was a child, children throw rocks.)

On October 11, 1938, Charley was transferred from Fergus Falls to the new Moose Lake State Hospital nearer his "home." At 8:50 A.M., on November 14, 1957, following a five-day bout with influenza, he died of a sudden coronary occlusion. All told, he spent nearly thirty of his fifty-four years behind the fences for "throwing rocks and sticks into the street." But maybe that was better than being buried for thirty years in the sweatshop laundry beneath the Hotel Solem.

My uncles Willie and Oscar were the inseparables of the family. Willie, born December 6, 1906, and Oscar, born April 11, 1908, were, besides being close brothers in a time sense, good friends who looked out for one another most of their lives. They also received more whippings from the old man than any of the rest of their siblings because they had the misfortune to come into the world at a time when their father's cruelty was at its peak, possibly the result of the combination of a midlife crisis, the loss of the farm near Moose Lake, and the undeniable fact that he was simply a mean sonofabitch.

When Oscar and Willie were about eight and nine years old respectively, the old man put them to work making cement blocks for the blacksmith shop he was building in Crosby. The labor, of course, was much too hard for children that age. They soon wandered off to pursue activities more to their liking. Enraged, the old man beat them, tethered them on a long chain to a tree like a couple of ante-bellum slaves and put them back to mixing sand and cement in a mortar box with a shovel and a hoe.

They remained at their task until their brother Swen, then about seventeen, came home from his shift in the iron mine. Swen unshackled the boys and told them to go play. The old man never said a word. He was afraid of Swen and not without cause. He knew instinctively, had he intervened, Swen probably would have killed him.

Of the nine boys in the family, Swen stuck it out at home the longest. Whereas the others left as soon as they could, Swen felt a responsibility to his mother and the younger children. He stayed in the mines to keep food on the table for them. He also kept a rein on the old man, saving his mother from more than one unprovoked beating.

Swen was the only one of the fourteen siblings who never attended school and never learned to read. (The others' school attendance varied from a few months to eight years. My father, Frank, had the most. Moving to Cloquet with Lucy, he eventually graduated from the eighth grade.) Swen, born with a mule's stubborn streak, decided the day he was to have begun the first grade that he didn't want any part of it. That was that. He didn't go. It's possible, with all the kids coming and going, no one realized he wasn't attending school. Most likely, though, nobody cared one way or the other. His only contact with the public education system that I know of was when he and my father went to the school in Crosby to complain to a principal who'd overzealously used a belt on their little brother, Oscar. They hustled the bully into the woods behind the school and converted him to the doctrine of nonviolence.

Swen could have gone far with an education. He was intelligent and a good worker. He eventually married a waitress by the name of Esther Hackman, a farm girl from near Brookston, Minnesota, who was employed at the Hotel Solem. They raised two fine sons. Swen spent forty-some years in the paper mill in Cloquet, ran a firewood business on the side and further supplemented those incomes with hunting and trapping. The only regret Swen ever voiced about not having attended school was his inability to read. In his retirement years he very much wanted to drive to the West Coast and visit my father, but unable to read a road map or to decipher the road signs and stubbornly not trusting his wife's ability to do so, he never made it.

On December 21, 1970, Swen went out to the garage behind his home to get his car. His wife heard the motor racing and went to see what was going on. She found Swen, age seventy-two, dead of a sudden heart attack, his body sprawled half in and half out of the automobile.

My uncles Willie and Oscar, on leaving Crosby, eventually found their way to Cloquet where they worked in the mills and kept the numerous barkeepers solvent. Oscar, like his brother Charley, had an ear for music. Self taught, he played the accordion and the harmonica. He could also take a violin bow and draw sweet arias from an ordinary carpenter's saw. His big problem was his choices of when to play. He usually felt an overpowering need to entertain when he was inebriated. Unfortunately, that was invariably at two or three o'clock in the morning.

Willie and Oscar lived for a time in a large Finnish boarding establishment for bachelors called Toivola House on Avenue F in Cloquet. It wasn't a fancy place, but it was scrub crazy, Finn clean and the food was good. It so happened, however, that Oscar returned home in the wee hours one morning and decided to introduce a little culture into everyone's life with a medley of tunes on his accordion. His efforts were not met with overwhelming appreciation, and he soon found himself, his accordion, and his personal effects outside on the curb.

With the eviction, the two brothers moved into a miserable woodshed-like shack behind their sister Ida's place on lower Tenth Street. One night, following an evening of debauchery, Oscar again decided to perform on his squeeze box. Willie, still miffed about losing their welcome at the Toivola House, was working the day shift at the paper mill and needed his sleep. He put an end to the impromptu concert quickly. The next day on my way to play with Willard Bodin, I passed my uncles' shack. Sticking out of the top of their trash can was the mangled remains of Oscar's accordion. Willie had taken a knife and slashed its bellows to ribbons.

We weren't living on Tenth Street anymore when shortly before World War II, word filtered through the family that Oscar was spending an inordinate amount of time at the Dairy Inn Ice Cream Parlor on Cloquet Avenue. The reaction of the clan was total disbelief. Oscar drinking milk shakes? His usual fare was at least ninety proof. It turned out that he was in love, smitten with one of the young waitresses. He was twelve years older than she, but they tied the knot and seemed happy. Seven months after the wedding, however, Oscar was drafted into the army.

With the completion of basic training, the groom was shipped directly to Iran for three long years. Assigned to the motor pool of the Nineteenth Station Hospital, he drove ambulances between the airport and the medical facility. The hospital handled some 10,000 patients during the war, both Russian soldiers injured fighting the Germans and American fliers wounded on bombing runs from England to Berlin and on to Poltava, U.S.S.R. When Oscar finally returned home, both he and his wife had lost interest in their marriage. Oscar went back to the bottle.

Private Oscar Carlson, U.S. Army 1942.

Willie, in the meantime, had also been drafted and sent in with the first wave onto the beaches of North Africa. Part of an artillery outfit, his unit was outflanked and eventually surrounded by Field Marshal Rommel's panzer divisions. After heavy fighting, out of ammunition and exhausted (Willie went to sleep beside his gun once and woke to find himself on the edge of a shell hole that hadn't been there when he shut his eyes), their officers surrendered them to the Germans.

Willie was taken to Italy and then Germany, spending a total of twenty-eight months as a prisoner. As the war in Europe wound down into its final days, Willie and his fellow captives were marched back and forth across Germany between the oncoming American troops on one side and the Russians on the other. Finally, one day their captors herded them into a woods and ordered them to stay down. Before long, someone noticed that the guards had all disappeared. The prisoners worked their way to a road and stumbled into an advance column of U.S. tanks and infantry.

At the time of his rescue, Willie, whose normal weight was about 175 pounds, scaled in at eighty-four. Needless to say, he had no love for Germans or anything remotely German. Parking a Volkswagen near Willie when he was in his cups was not a good idea.

On his return to Cloquet after the war, Willie went back to his job at the paper mill but quit when they refused to take him off rotating shift work. He took a job on a turkey farm near Aitkin, Minnesota, but soon decided that nursemaiding poultry was not his

PrivateWilliam "Willie" Carlson, U.S. Army 1942.

forte. Locating his brother Oscar on skid row in Duluth, they coasted together into the unreal world of alcoholism. Eventually, they moved into a mission dedicated to helping derelicts and earned their keep as jacks-of-all-trades for the organization. At one time, we heard they were even giving testimonial sermons to their fellow unfortunates. (That bit of news sent a shockwave through their siblings that far exceeded the trauma instilled by Oscar's earlier milk-shake incident.)

Willie finally reached a point where his body rebelled against the abuse he was pouring into it. Sick and despondent, he took a hard look at himself and put aside the bottle for good. He stayed on at the mission, however, and looked after Oscar. In early 1973, Oscar was diagnosed as having advanced cancer of the prostate. He died on October 1, in a Duluth hospital at age sixty-five. Willie, having squirreled away a few dollars from his social security pension and odd jobs, purchased two grave sites side by side in the Cloquet cemetery and took care of all the arrangements.

With Oscar gone, Willie rented a tiny hole of a room at the Hotel Solem. My father and I visited with him for a few minutes in 1974 on a quick trip from the West Coast. Years of neglect had reduced the hotel to a skid row hovel of leaky plumbing, accumulated grime, and hopeless disrepair. The first thing Willie said when he saw us was, "God, how I miss that boy!"

In the spring of 1980, Willie came down with what he surmised was a bad cold. When symptoms persisted, he went to see a doctor and learned he had inoperable lung cancer. He immediately made his own funeral arrangements and put all his affairs in order. He died on June 18, at age seventy-three and was laid to rest alongside Oscar—an inseparable pair to the end.

My uncle John also served in the army during World War II. In spite of a history of alcoholism (he was sent to state hospital at least twice to dry out) and being over forty years old, he was drafted and served as a private with the Eighty-fourth Infantry Training Battalion in California. After a little more than a year in the army, the military decided it didn't need the older men, and John was honorably discharged with the provision that he enter defense work.

John had stayed sober in the army, but back in the real world (he worked in an aircraft plant in Los Angeles), he returned to his thirsty ways. Drinking, he didn't eat. His body weakened and he developed pneumonia. He died in the Sawtelle Veterans Administration Hospital in Los Angeles on August 2, 1945, at age forty-four. John's brother Oscar's wife, who was living in the Los Angeles area at the time, visited him shortly before he passed away. She was the only visitor he had. . . .

15

More Tenth Street

On October 25, 1932, I was struck down in the street by an automobile.

It was a time of Indian summer in northern Minnesota, a time of crisp, frosty mornings, dazzling, clear sunny days, and sharp, starry, moonlit nights—an invigorating leaf-crunching time of year marred only by the need to attend school. The evening of the accident, my father had gone jacklighting with a man who was desperate to put meat on his family's table. The fellow had managed to come up with two .32 caliber rifle shells but had no weapon for them. Learning that my father owned a .32 Winchester, he suggested they pool their resources. The man dropped his wife off at our house, and the two men left to stake out a clearing and wait for deer that, being nocturnal creatures, bed down in the brush by day and come out in the evening to gambol on open turf.

My mother didn't know her visitor very well, but following the time-honored social mores of the community, she put on the coffee pot. For some reason, which was very much unlike her, Mom was caught without the usual cake or cookies to serve her guest (I may have had something to do with the situation). From a hidden cache squirreled away in her cupboards, she dug out a half-dollar piece and packed my friend Bozo and me off to Blomberg's Store, a mom-and-pop grocery four blocks east on Cloquet Avenue that stayed open in the evenings.

As Bozo and I climbed Tenth Street hill and turned toward Blomberg's, the last pink glow of the setting sun highlighted the blazing colors of the fall foliage veiling the bluff on the north side of the St. Louis River. We hurried along, anticipating our purchase, or more exactly, our impending share. Since most bakery items were made from scratch at home, we thought store-bought was something special.

97

Reaching Eleventh Street, we entered the intersection without bothering to look for traffic; at that hour of the evening in 1932 most folks were sitting down to dinner or listening to their radios. I was on the Cloquet Avenue side and about three-fourths of the way across Eleventh Street when Bozo grabbed my left arm and yelled, "Look out!" I turned my head to the right. Less than three feet away were two dim, oncoming headlights, and I was between them.

To this day I have absolutely no recollection of the car striking me. I saw the headlights, and then I was lying on my stomach in the ditch on the east side of the street. I sat up and looked around. The car, driven by Mr. Paul Pirho, the local tailor, was skidding to a dusty halt about thirty yards down the hill. Bozo was lying flat on his back in the middle of the road, his head resting on a big rock, his eyes squeezed shut. He was screaming. I saw two men crossing Cloquet Avenue toward us on the run. Half dazed, I started to get up. There was an immediate crackling, knuckle-popping sound as a lightning-fast pain shot through the length of my right leg. Dropping backward onto my rear, I began to cry.

The two men coming across Cloquet Avenue reached us and, in a hurried conference, decided to take us to Raiter Brothers' Hospital two blocks west on the corner of Ninth Street. Snatching us up like two armloads of firewood, they took off at a quick trot. I don't remember the car's driver being on the scene at all. Maybe he froze behind the steering wheel. As we approached Tenth Street, I told the man carrying me to take me home and pointed at our house. He started down the hill, but his partner, toting the still screaming Bozo, yelled, "Where are you going?"

"This kid says he lives in that first house and wants to go home," my rescuer answered.

"To hell with that! Take him to Raiters'!"

Once at the hospital, we were hustled into a small room furnished with a couple of white enameled examining tables. Bozo was laid, still screaming with his eyes squeezed shut, on one; I was deposited in a sitting position with my legs dangling over the edge on the other. Dr. Roy Raiter appeared from somewhere inside the building and calmly took over. I'd stopped crying on the way to the hospital. My leg had quit hurting, possibly from shock, but I managed to work up a quiet snuffle for sympathy purposes. Dr. Roy checked the screaming Bozo and had him wheeled from the room. Turning his attention to me, he shined his ophthalmoscope into my eyes and asked if I hurt anywhere. I told him my right leg ached a little. Dr.

Roy carefully unlaced my boot (the popular footwear for boys at the time were leather boots that laced almost to the knee and had a small pocketknife scabbard on the outside of one leg). As Dr. Roy gingerly slipped the boot off my foot, I saw Mr. Pirho standing in the hallway outside the room. He was wringing his hands and seemed near nervous collapse. He looked ill, his face gray as a "before" sheet in one of the Fels Naptha laundry soap magazine ads. At that moment my mother and Mrs. Erickson, summoned by the two men who had carried us to the hospital, arrived on the scene. Poor Mr. Pirho, on the verge of tears, told the ladies: "I didn't see them! I didn't even know I'd hit them until I saw their legs fly up over the windshield!"

My mother, very calm, asked Dr. Roy (the Raiter brothers—Franklin, Roy, and Roscoe—were always addressed by their first names) how I was. He answered that his preliminary examination indicated a fractured leg. Other than that, and a few minor abrasions from skidding along the gravel street, I seemed okay. He rigged my leg in a kind of basket affair and said they would X-ray in the morning and the do whatever needed to be done. As they wheeled me to my hospital room, I remembered the half-dollar piece—it was still clutched tightly in my left hand. I gave it to my mother. Neither she nor Dr. Roy could suppress a chuckle.

Sometime during the night, both my folks looked in on me. I was heavily sedated, but when I realized they were there, I asked Dad, "Did you get any?" He held up two fingers, and I drifted back to sleep.

In the early hours before dawn, Dr. Roy tapped Bozo's spine to relieve pressure from a hemorrhage on his brain. After a few days convalescence, he was discharged from the hospital, none the worse from the experience.

X-rays showed that my right leg was fractured in three places between the knee and the ankle. Dr. Roy said the leather boot, acting as a splint, saved the leg from more serious damage. He encased the limb in plaster from my crotch to my ankle and ordered me to stay home and not put any weight on it for six weeks.

When the cast was finally removed, my right leg looked like an elongated yellow banana, totally devoid of life and muscle. My mother was instructed to work my leg, bending it at the knee several times a day until my brain regained control of the withered limb and I could move it myself. Today, the process would be called physical therapy and require the services of a highly educated, well-paid professional. Then, it was just exercise, and mother worked for free.

The leg recovered completely and has never caused me any further problems. Returning to school after the long convalescence was a different story. My group was so far ahead of me, I didn't have the remotest chance of catching up. I tried, but there was no doubt in my mind or anybody else's that I was the class dunce. If I hadn't figured it out for myself, there were at least a couple of snooty girls who loved to go out of their way to make certain I was informed.

Added to the school problems, I began to have severe abdominal pains. I would be feeling perfectly well when, without warning, my guts would cramp into knots and I'd break out in a cold sweat, unable to move from a squatting, doubled-over position until the seizure passed. This went on for quite some time, but I never told anyone because I didn't want any more hospital stays. Then, one Saturday night as I climbed out of the circular washtub set in front of our kitchen range for the weekly cleansing ritual (you took a bath on Saturday night whether you needed it or not), my mother noticed that my scrotum was bulging enormously on one side. I'd been aware of it for several days but said nothing for the same reason I never mentioned the cramps.

The next morning, early, I was back in Dr. Roy's office (although it was Sunday, he was at the hospital making his rounds). His diagnosis was hernia and into surgery I went. It turned out that my intestine had been partially strangulated since the accident. Dr. Roy removed about nine inches of gut that had turned black, and I began the recovery process all over again.

With the new absence from the classroom, school authorities suggested to my folks that I give up for that session and re-enroll in the second grade at the beginning of the next school year. It turned out to be the best thing that could have happened to me academically. I'd started school too young and had had to struggle constantly to keep up with my class. In the year I sat out, the neurons in my brain cells had a chance to synapse or whatever they do as one matures, and school was never a problem again. Average grades came without effort, better grades took very little.

My increased scholarship, however, was the only good to come from the accident. Physically, I couldn't seem to snap back. I gagged through countless bottles of cod liver oil and other touted revitalizing tonics without avail. I was weak and listless, and when the next Minnesota winter came on, every bug that came down the road decided I was ready for harvest. Dr. Franklin Raiter sat up with me one whole night, pouring scalding black coffee laced with butter down my throat as I strangled with whooping cough. I had two bouts with pneumonia, and both times my chest was fried with countless mustard plasters. Why I didn't develop scar tissue, I'll never know. Then, chronic sinusitis and related ear problems set in, which led to two mastoid surgeries, one massive sinus operation that left bone splinters working their way out of my gums for years, plus numerous eardrum lancings and untold numbers of sinus irrigations that hurt terribly and were effective for thirty minutes or so. In short, I was a surgeon's dream—take out everything but leave just enough to pay the bill—and a nightmare for my parents who worried over me and watched the medical costs inundate them. Penicillin had been discovered in 1928 but wasn't available to the public. Pharmaceutical companies refused to produce it, because they couldn't get a clear patent to turn it into big bucks. If there is any justice, those responsible for that greedy decision should spend eternity in hell having hot lead poured into their ears and other less convenient orifices.

All the surgeries, treatments, and illnesses naturally took their toll. From grades two through four, I was a puny, sickly kid not given much chance for survival by the tongue-flapping small town tale-bearers who deemed to know all. I fooled them.

I missed a lot of school but managed to get in enough time to progress. After a bout with one bug or another, my folks would both pitch in and tutor me in the basics. Dad was good at math, Mom at language arts. They soon had me doing as well as the average kid who'd been in school all the time. I actually surpassed many of my peers in general knowledge and reading skills, thanks to the Cloquet Public Library and a helpful, caring librarian by the name of Miss Kennedy. With little else to do during the long hours while my folks worked at the Hotel Solem, I read widely and became addicted to books.

Forced to spend protracted periods each day by myself never bothered me except once. Cloquet was a town where hardly anyone ever locked their doors. We trusted one another. Besides, most house locks were of the standard variety that worked with a universal skeleton key. Your key fit your neighbors' doors and vice versa. Anyway, one morning I was alone in the house, lounging around in my bathrobe and slippers. I was kneeling on a kitchen chair, watching icicles hanging from the edge of the roof outside getting longer and longer as they dripped in a premature January (c. 1934) thaw. Suddenly, the back door burst open and a big, seedy-looking character bundled in a dirty Mackinaw coat, a gray cap with the earflaps down covering his head, barged into the house. He slammed the door behind him and plunged unsteadily into the kitchen. Jerking a chair out from under the table, the intruder plopped himself down heavily between me and the way out to the rear of the house. He looked around bleary-eyed and shouted, "Elsie!" Getting no answer, he yelled again, "Elsie . . . , goddamn woman!"

I'd seen enough drunks to know he was one, but knowing that didn't make him any less formidable. "Nobody named Elsie lives here," I managed to squeak.

He looked at me, struggled to focus his bloodshot eyes, and, I think, realized for the first time that I was there. Taking in my night clothes, he roared, "What's the matta you?"

"I've been sick," I sniffled like the trapped mouse to the lion, but he wasn't listening.

He turned toward the entryway to our living room and bellowed, "Elsie! Goddamn woman!" With that, he pitched forward onto his face, sprawling out the width of the kitchen floor.

I was terrified. I looked out the window to the back of the hotel. Although my folks periodically checked our house from the hotel's windows, I didn't see a soul. I made a run for our front entryway. Ice had formed along the bottom of the storm door. I couldn't budge it.

There was no choice—to escape, I would have to step over the prostrate intruder. It took all the courage I could muster. I eased myself on tiptoes over his inert body. He stirred. Certain he was going to grab my legs, I leaped and bolted out the back door.

I don't remember plunging through the icy water, slush, and snow that covered the ground between our house and the back stairway to the hotel, but I must have. My father was working at the huge kitchen stove when I burst in on him. He stared questioningly, and I blurted out, "There's a man in our house!"

"Who?" he asked, putting down the skillet he'd been holding.

"I don't know! He's laying on the floor."

At that, my father was on his way. The kitchen staff and I watched from the windows as he bounded up our back steps and entered the house. A few seconds later the intruder came flying out, and I mean flying. He never touched the steps; he dived like a shotgunned goose into the yard, belly-flopping in a geyser of ice water and slush. As he flailed about trying to gain his feet and orient himself, losing one of his red rubber galoshes in the process, my uncle Nick, totally oblivious as to what was happening, came down the walk alongside the house on his way home from an all-night poker game. From where I was watching in the hotel, I didn't see one word of communication pass between Nick and my father, who had now reached the top of the steps in pursuit of the drunk, but somehow they decided it was Nick's turn to get a piece of the guy.

Nick grabbed the hapless trespasser by the back of his collar and kicked his tail all the way up the hill to Cloquet Avenue. He was still booting him as they passed from sight around the corner of the Leb Theater. I never saw the man again, but his red rubber shoe reappeared from under the snow with the final spring thaw.

After my grandmother Carlson died in 1932, some of my enforced confinements due to illnesses were brightened by the chance to observe my grandfather Nicolai, the old man, carry on a constant campaign to acquire female companionship.

Lord knows how many bastards he sired during his lifetime, but my guess is it was a considerable number. In his younger days, he worked away from his family a good deal and was still sniffing around long past the time when most men have all but forgotten what it was they used to do. My aunt Alena once told me that the old man kept his house much warmer than most people because he didn't like to be cold. The truth is he usually had some old lady romping around the place naked, a feat considerably more difficult to accomplish in a chilly environment.

The old man would advertise for eligible (that simply means they had to be breathing) ladies in the Finnish language newspapers in the Twin Cities. I don't know what he wrote them after the initial contact, but his line must have been good. They usually came into town on the Greyhound bus. I quickly learned that when my grandfather hurried up Tenth Street in his only dress suit toward Cloquet Avenue and the bus stop, he would, in all likelihood, soon be escorting some lady back down the hill. They came in all shapes and sizes, their meager belongings held in battered suitcases, shopping bags, and worn cardboard boxes kept together with frayed sisal. Hope, desperation, and sometimes fear was mirrored in their faces. They were women treated badly by life, grasping for a last chance of happiness or security. A few got off the bus, took one look at the old man, and climbed back on. Others came down the hill to stay anywhere from a few minutes to a few weeks before trudging back alone.

In the summer of 1937, a widow from Annandale, Minnesota, moved in with my grandfather. A woman who had given birth to thirteen children in her first marriage, she talked the old man into moving to Annandale so she could be closer to her kids. My grandfather soon decided "they kept their house too cold," however, and brought the lady back to Cloquet. They were living, as the saying goes, without benefit of clergy, which didn't sit well with my aunt Alena. She threw a tizzy, and the old man let her make the arrangements with the minister of the Finnish Lutheran Church. He and the woman marched to the altar. The wedding took place September 16, 1937. Alena was the only one in attendance, but she threw rice on the newlyweds as they left the church. The nuptials must have been followed by a strenuous honeymoon. On November 20, 1937, two months and four days after the wedding ceremony and sixteen days short of his seventy-eighth birthday, the old man died . . . in bed.

The funeral was a well-attended affair. At least twelve of the old man's children, their families, and a surprising number of obviously saddened elderly women paid their respects. The minister, overjoyed to see the size of the turnout, waxed eloquent, praising the deceased for his outstanding qualities as a loving father and husband. He faltered a little, however, when a barely audible male voice from the rear of the church intoned, "Bu-ull-shi-it!"

16

Yee-Haw! San Antonio!

Nineteen thirty-six was the beginning of the end of my seemingly endless health problems. Autumn had barely settled in before my round robin bouts with ear and sinus infections began setting me up for the coup de grace. Rundown, skinny, and totally weakened from the health turmoils of the previous winter, it was becoming obvious that my chances of surviving another frost-bound season in boreal Minnesota would be dicey at best. The old crone soothsayers were nodding sagely to one another while mentally crinkling the black crepe.

The doctors Raiter, having exhausted the repertoire of mustard plasters, nose and ear drops, heat lamps (I set my hair on fire more than once), fever powders, and simple voodoo of the general practitioner of the day, had long since packed me off to a Dr. Knapp, an eyes, ears, and nose specialist in Duluth. By the fall of 1936, Dr. Knapp had performed most of the previously mentioned surgeries on my ears and sinuses and shoved all the known hardware and nostrums of his trade up my nose. It was a toss-up as to who or what was going to kill me—the medical profession or infection. Finally, Dr. Knapp threw in the towel and suggested, "Take him to Texas. Maybe a change of climate will help."

I'm sure Dr. Knapp's prescription was a real heart-wrenching blow for my mother. After years of moving from one rental to another suffering pangs of conscience during the lawless era, and struggling with abject poverty in the early part of the Great Depression, she and my father had their own home on Tenth Street, Dad had a steady job at the paper mill, and she was happily involved with church affairs and Sunday school teaching. Except for worrying over me, Mom was comfortably settled in as a typical Minnesota housewife only to have it all blow up in her face with the words "take him to Texas."

My father wasn't overly perturbed by the doctor's pronouncement. Dad was a man who liked to be on the go. He delighted in change. I know that the steady job at the paper mill, the routine predictable surety of each day, week in and week out, was an unwelcomed tether. He didn't complain about it; he just would have preferred to forego the numbing security of it all and kick off the traces.

Texas bound, my folks sold our house and furnishings to Dad's sister Alena and her husband, John Becklund. Helen Solem, Hans' and Lucy's eldest daughter, had graduated from St. Olaf College in Northfield, Minnesota, the previous spring and was rewarded with a new 1936 Plymouth sedan from her parents. Like most young people sprung from the tedium of higher education, Helen wanted to travel. Hans, concerned about his daughter touring alone, gave his blessing to a trip provided she make Texas her destination (he'd purchased some property there sight unseen and wanted her to check it out) and let my father share the driving. He also insisted that another cousin, one of Hilda's daughters, join the group so Helen wouldn't be alone on the return trip. Shipping some things via the railroad and packing everything else we hadn't sold along with the two girls' gear into the green Plymouth, we headed south.

Without any pressing schedule and unsure if we would ever again be returning to the North, we traveled at a leisurely pace, visiting Dad's sister Olga in Menomonie, Wisconsin, and my mother's people in the Racine-Kenosha area. From Kenosha, we headed for Chicago to visit my father's youngest brother, Jalmer.

Jalmer, the last born of the fourteen Carlson children, was four years younger than Alena, who had advised him in his late teens to get out of Cloquet and find someplace where he'd have a chance for a future. Jalmer heeded her advice and moved to Chicago where he found employment with one of the nation's major candy manufacturers.

Jalmer and his wife LaVerne hadn't been married very long when we barged in on them. They lived in a tenement house on DesPlains Street near the site of the historically infamous Haymarket Riot. From the outside, the building resembled a prop for a "Dead End" movie—bricks walls covered with the grime of decades, laundry drying on the fire escapes, the street in front a mass of broken, worn bricks—but inside, Jalmer and his wife had completely renovated their flat. There was new wallpaper, fresh paint, and comfortable furnishings. Many of the other apartments in the tenement seemed to be occupied by LaVerne's relatives, giving the place the semblance of housing one large family. The odor of boiled cabbage wafted throughout the building at dinner time while shouted conversations in an olio of English, Lithuanian, and Polish echoed in the halls and stairwells. Jalmer confided that following his and LaVerne's wedding, he hardly saw his bride for three days, what with all the Slavic-style celebrating throughout the neighborhood.

Jalmer gave us the short Cook's Tour of Chicago. I got to stand on the corner of State and Madison where, it is said, if you wait long enough, you'll see everybody you know. (I was only there a few minutes but was disappointed. I didn't recognize a single person.) We visited Maxwell Street where the Jewish merchants in their black hats and temple curls had dragged all their wares onto the sidewalks, giving the area the likeness of a gigantic yard sale. We also made a cursory visit to the Biograph Theater, driving slowly past the spot where John Dillinger, betrayed by the Lady in Red, was gunned down by G-men under the command of Pontius Purvis.

We spent two nights in Chicago before continuing on our southerly course. (I saw Jalmer once after that in 1988. We both attended a family reunion in San Diego, California. A widower, he lived out his final days with one of his children in Chicago where he died on July 3, 1991, age eighty-two.)

Our journey continued through Missouri, Arkansas, and finally into Texas. We rented tent cabins (wooden floors and sides with white canvas tops) in Dallas, spending one full day visiting the Texas Centennial Exposition. Knowing absolutely nothing about Texas history, I couldn't relate to many of the exhibits, but I do remember Sally Rand:

> Sally Rand,
> She lost her fans;
> Give them back,
> You nasty man!

We caught her matinee performance, and I must say she certainly could manipulate those fans. I don't think I blinked once throughout the entire show, but I never saw anything except feathers.

I rode my first rollercoaster that same day. Texans, striving for bigger and better, outdid themselves on that one. It was the only carnival ride on which I ever refused seconds. The experience ended with me crouched down on the floor of the car wondering if it would ever stop.

We arrived in San Antonio, our tentative destination, on a muggy, sunny afternoon. My folks rented the first furnished apartment they could find, and Dad went shopping for a car, bringing home a tan 1932 Chevrolet sedan with red wire wheels, twin chromed horns up front, and two spare tires mounted in the forward fenders. It was a beauty! The two girls spent a couple of days with us looking over the city before continuing on their way to Mexico. I never heard what Hans Solem's reaction was to the news that his daughter was going to Mexico, but I'll wager he came close to swallowing his cigar.

More or less settled in, I was enrolled in the fifth grade at the Robert B. Green Elementary School, and my father went in search of employment.

We soon discovered that our apartment building was definitely in a low, low-income neighborhood. The economy was tight in Minnesota, but San Antonio was the first place I ever saw children scrounging through garbage containers for something to eat. Gangs of youngsters would pick through the cans along the street in front of our building every morning, wolfing down anything remotely edible. On Tenth Street in Cloquet, there was a pale, tiny wisp of a blonde girl who cried a lot and ate rust she picked off the wheels of her father's old Essex automobile, but never garbage. It was years before anyone figured out she was simply anemic and answering her body's demand for iron.

Most of the people in our building were Hispanics who simply ignored us. I seriously doubt that we were in any danger, but my mother, accustomed to the blue-eyed, winter-white faces of Minnesotans, felt extremely uneasy surrounded by dark eyes and swarthy complexions. The fact that some of the men had the given name Jesus, a name often mentioned in San Antonio news stories of murder and mayhem, didn't help much either. When the rent came due, we moved into a duplex in a slightly more predominantly Anglo neighborhood. We were there exactly one month before moving again.

This time it was a problem with the landlady. She was a thief. We first became aware of her taking ways when we observed her rustling her neighbors' poultry. In order to survive, many families within San Antonio's city limits kept chickens and even dairy cows. The fowl were generally free to forage for themselves while the bovines were staked out along the roadsides during the day to graze on the public domain. Anyway, our landlady had a big, black Labrador named Nigger, and she'd trained the dog to fetch chickens on command without killing or bruising them. He'd simply hold a bird down with one paw until he could get a firm but gentle grip with his teeth and bring it to his mistress. Politicians of the time, vying for public office, were promising "a new car in every garage and a chicken in every pot." A quick twist of the bird's neck, and our landlady had the contents for her pot. The woman's larcenous ways didn't concern us, however, until things began to disappear from our cupboards in our absence. We moved.

By this time, my father had scoured San Antonio, Houston, Galveston, and Corpus Christi without finding even a possibility of a job. Facing the realities of the situation, Dad wrote to his former boss at the paper mill in Cloquet and was offered his old job back. Having to support two residences, Mom's and mine in San Antonio and someplace for himself in Cloquet, he and my mother found a very inexpensive shack on West Sayer Street just off Pleasanton Road in the Harlandale section of south San Antonio. Settling us in (it didn't take much—my bed was the backseat out of the Chevrolet, hauled into the shack each evening and out each morning), Dad boarded a train for the winter blasts of Minnesota.

I hadn't been exactly ecstatic about attending Robert B. Green Elementary School. The administration had instituted a system of overzealous student monitors who diligently policed the place and delighted in reporting rule infractions, an easy task because they had more chicken regulations to enforce than a military academy. My very first recess found me in the principal's office charged with "jumping on another student's back." I couldn't believe it. We'd just been playing, working off a little excess energy. In Cloquet, our greatest recess joy was to kick the hell out of each other's shins in unorganized soccer games, and nobody complained. Moving to West Sayer Street, I left Mr. Green's memorial without regrets and enrolled at Harlandale Elementary School on Flores Street with my kind of people.

The Harlandale suburb of San Antonio was really nothing but a rundown, pastoral, small town satellite of the big city. Most of the cross streets, including West Sayer, were graveled, and there were lots of weed-covered fields and vacant areas for play. At least half the kids went barefoot to school (I once loaned my shoes to a friend so he could take part in a school play).

I've read that early immigrants to Texas, folks from Tennessee and Kentucky who followed Stephen Austin to the promised land, constructed their residences as a series of small rooms connected by long, open breezeways called dog runs to beat the summer's oppressive heat. Our shack on West Sayer Street was all dog run. I could lie on my car seat at night and see the stars through the cracks between the boards of the walls. Plumbing consisted of one cold-water tap in the kitchen sink and a one-holer out back. Rattlesnakes abounded in the neighborhood. Although I never saw a live one, I did see several shortly after they'd been killed. We always poked about the outhouse with a long stick before getting too comfortable. Small lizards flourished outdoors and were good natural thermometers. If they skittered across the road with their tails up, it was hot; tails down and dragging, pleasantly warm; and cool to cold weather drove them to their holes and out of sight.

Spiders, horned toads, and other reptiles were also in good supply. Each morning our kitchen sink contained several black widow spiders in search of water. Once, we ran the Chevrolet over a fat water moccasin where Pleasanton Road threaded through a swampy area a few miles south of where we lived. Alligators were common in San Antonio River, sometimes wandering into the city itself. I remember seeing a picture in the *San Antonio Light* newspaper of two Bexar County sheriff's deputies holding a 'gator on a pole between them. Early morning swimmers in a downtown section of the river had complained that something was bumping into them. The reptile was slightly more than six feet long.

There were about forty kids in my fifth grade class at Harlandale Elementary, some well into puberty. With no compulsory attendance laws in Texas at that time, a number of the students had taken occasional protracted sabbaticals to pick cotton or fruit with their families, taking up where they'd left off when they decided to return. Approximately a third of the group was of Mexican heritage, some not long north of the Rio Grande.

(Being a gringo and a damyankee to boot, I thought I might have problems, but I was never aware of any animosity directed my way. The class was a well-behaved group unencumbered by divisive cliques or special interest groups whose existence depends on excluding others. Everyone in the room treated each other and the teacher, Miss Livingston, with respect. Miss Livingston, in turn, did a good job presenting the basic three r's in spite of being handicapped by shortages of books and other elemental teaching materials. Minnesota schools were far better supplied than those I attended in Texas.)

With gasoline selling for eleven cents a gallon (none of this nine-tenths of a cent baloney on the end), my mother and I spent our weekends seeing the sights. We visited the historical attractions: the Alamo, the Spanish Governor's Palace, the missions, and my favorite place, Brackenridge Park. Not big on historical relics at that stage of my life, I preferred the park's large, rambling wooded expanses with its zoo and free burro rides for kids. Sometimes we drove out to Randolph Field, the West Point of the Air, to watch the free air shows put on for the public by the military.

San Antonio was an army town. Several Army Air Force bases ringed the city, and Fort Sam Houston was practically downtown. High school R.O.T.C. was big on the aristocratic north side where upperclassmen strutted proudly in their officers' pinks and Sam Browne belts; it was nonexistent in Harlandale. Carnival or Fiesta Week in the spring featured daily parades throughout the city, giving the military establishment an opportunity to show its stuff.

Fiesta Week, for reasons I've never quite understood, always turned into a ritual bloodletting among rival high schools. Each evening throughout the festival period, gangs of students roamed the city's core area, battling each other and the police with knives, clubs, hammers and the like. They didn't seem to bother noncombatant bystanders; at least, my mother and I were never threatened or molested as we shared the sidewalks with roving hordes of free-lance gladiators. The closest I came to being embroiled in a melee was being run down by two very hefty black ladies. Mom and I were strolling through the carnival midway temporarily occupying the Mexican open market site near the city center when a fight broke out. I never saw the brawl. The first thing I knew, two women burst from the crowd in front of me like a pair of stampeding buffalo. They bowled me over like a tire-chasing dog caught under a speeding automobile. I was back on my feet, brushing straw and sawdust off my body when they returned to apologize. Out of breath, the talker of the two gasped, "Lawdy! One of does gennel'mens had a knife. We was so skeered, we just got!"

With the approach of summer, it was time for us to leave Texas and head for Cloquet. Eager to get underway, my mother arranged for me to withdraw from school a couple of weeks before the year was officially over, and we pointed the Chevrolet northward.

My father had "taught" my mother to drive during the moonshine running days. On a visit to one of his stills, he drove Mom a couple of miles beyond its location in St. Louis County, turned the car around, and retraced their route. Satisfied that they hadn't been followed, Dad, without stopping, stepped out onto the running board. He had Mom slip behind the wheel and told her not to stop until she got back to Cloquet. Then he jumped off.

Mom, concerned that she might kill the engine if she slowed down, rammed the accelerator to the floor and mostly kept it there until she arrived home. It was her only driving lesson, and she took to speed like an Englishman to tea. Many years later at the age of seventy-plus, she was still laying rubber on the streets and keeping the engine running.

Leaving San Antonio, we crossed Texas and stopped for the night just over the border in Oklahoma. The next night found us in Fort Scott, Kansas. Up early, we pounded the road for twelve hundred miles, stopping for nothing but gasoline and food until we reached Cloquet—this in a day when roads were narrow two lanes with ninety degree turns at each farmer's section. My momma could drive!

17

Settling In

Thomas Wolfe said, "You can't go home again." Before Wolfe, Kahil Gibran wrote in *The Prophet*, "For life goes not backward or tarries with yesterday." I'd never heard of either Wolfe or Gibran in the spring of 1937, but I became acutely aware of the truth they were trying to convey.

When my mother and I rolled into Cloquet, we went directly to the house on Avenue F where my father was renting a single sleeping room, taking most of his meals at Dubie's boarding establishment on Cloquet Avenue. By the time the preliminary greetings were over, it was mid-afternoon, and my folks decided I needed to go out and play to work off the weariness of the long trip. I wasn't in any big hurry to leave, but they practically shoved me out the door, suggesting I go back to the old neighborhood on Tenth Street and find my pals.

As I passed the Leb Theater and turned off Cloquet Avenue down Tenth Street, the first thing I saw was our house; but, it wasn't our house anymore, it was my aunt Alena's. Right then I knew that, for me, Tenth Street was never going to be the same. No one was home at Alena's except Jack, the dog I'd raised from a tiny pup. The short-haired, brown and white mixture of several varieties of terriers and possibly a wandering bulldog was sunning himself on the back steps. He seemed to know me and condescended to have his ears scratched, but he wasn't my dog anymore. Instead of following me when I left, he sighed contentedly, stretched, and went back to his interrupted dreams.

My old buddy Bozo Erickson and his sisters didn't seem to know exactly what to do with me. I certainly wasn't a stranger, but we all sensed that I didn't belong there anymore. (It may seem strange to outsiders, but if you haven't shared the rigors of the latest northern Minnesota winter with your neighbors, you're no longer one of them. To be welcomed back into the fold completely, one must don the woolies and risk nine months of frostbite to be reinstated.) The Ericksons thought my Texas accent was hilarious. I'd sucked up the twang complete with "y'alls" and "thataways" like a dry bar rag soaking up dregs on the first swipe of the day. Embarrassed and somewhat miffed by the reception, I said I'd be back and wandered on my way through the old neighborhood. Nothing seemed to have changed, but I felt somehow relieved when I'd climbed back up the hill to Cloquet Avenue without visiting any more of the old gang. Although I didn't know it at the time, a small but important nurturing stage of my life had come to an end.

With that short walk back up the hill, close ties with the old crowd were history. We did, of course, meet on the streets and in school but as friendly acquaintances, not intimates. Over the years, most of the group grew up and moved on. New east-west streets eventually divided the neighborhood into neat, sterile rectangles. Kallios, or Little Woods, became a commercial area of auto shops and storage buildings. Old houses were torn down to be replaced by paved parking spaces and gasoline pumps. The neatly stacked lumber piles west of Ninth Street gave way to a park with Little League ball fields—super adult-organized recreation supplanting the creative give and take of children's play. Our house, still owned by my aunt Alena, remains standing. Ericksons' home belongs to someone else. The old man's place is a small rental, his blacksmith shop converted into a one-car garage. All of the outhouses we used to tip on Halloween have succumbed to modern plumbing. The Leb Theater building, once a place of magic and adventure for a nickel on Saturday afternoons, now houses a department store.

Of the old gang, Willard Bodin was the only one who didn't make it to adulthood. On October 9, 1939, he and another boy, Fred Arbuckle, played hooky from school to hunt rabbits in the woods across the St. Louis River north of town. They were sharing a single-shot .22 caliber rifle that the Arbuckle boy was carrying when tragedy struck. Climbing a slight rise, Willard, in the lead, saw a real or imagined rabbit. Turning to his friend, he reached for the weapon, grasping it by the muzzle. The rifle discharged in the boys' hands, the bullet entering Willard's abdominal area.

Terrified and in considerable pain, Willard ran for about a mile with Fred right behind him. They reached the river, coming out of the woods just across from a crew of men working a raft of logs for the paper company. Using a rowboat, a couple of the men came for the boys while someone else was sent to call for an ambulance. Willard was taken to Raiters' Hospital but almost immediately transferred to a better-equipped facility in Duluth.

Willard hung on for three days, but without the availability of antibiotics, peritonitis set in, and he died.

The day after Mom and I returned to Cloquet, my folks rented a house on Cloquet Avenue between Fifteenth and Sixteenth Streets, its backyard separated from my uncle Swen's home on Avenue C by an alley.

Swen was in the process of building a new saw rig, a trailered machine with a Model A Ford engine powering a circular saw. Although Swen couldn't read, he had an inborn talent for mechanical things, a natural aptitude shared to one degree or another by most of the Carlson brothers. (My father, an excellent hand with tools himself, always maintained that his brother John was the best of the lot. He claimed that John, a man with less than a third grade education, given access to the proper equipment, could construct an engine from a solid block of steel.) I was attracted to Swen's project and must have been an eleven-year-old nuisance, but Swen never complained. He was very patient and took time to answer all of my questions. He would have made a good teacher.

Swen was also something of a seat-of-the-pants psychologist although I doubt that he had ever heard of one. When his first-born, Bobby, was a toddler, the boy became attached to a security blanket with a satin binding that he kept constantly to his face. Bobby and his "dundee" as he called it were inseparable, and it wasn't long before his mother, Esther, had gone through the whole routine including cutting the blanket in two so half could be laundered while the kid clung tenaciously to the other.

Swen didn't say much about the "dundee" business, but I suspect the whole thing smacked of unmanliness on Bobby's part and didn't sit well. In spite of his misgivings, however, Swen let things ride until one sloppy, muddy day during the spring thaw when Bobby managed to drag both halves of his precious blanket through the muck. Esther, torn between her Finnish obsession with cleanliness and the psychic needs of her young son, was on the verge of tears when Swen decided enough was enough. Very calmly, he took Bobby, clutching his "dundee" like a drowning man with half a waterlogged life ring, by the hand and descended into the basement of their home. Without a word, Swen opened the door of the huge furnace dominating the center of the room. Both father and son silently watched the roaring flames for a long moment. Still without any discussion, Swen eased the "dundee" from Bobby's grasp and tossed it into the fire. Waiting until the blanket was entirely consumed in the inferno, Swen shut the furnace door and said to Bobby, "No more 'dundee.'" The kid never mentioned it again.

We remained in the house on Cloquet Avenue through the summer, but Dad wanted out of there before winter set in. The place, although a reasonably nice old home, was uninsulated, and Dad had visions of his wages going up the chimney trying to keep the building livable.

We moved just after Halloween 1937. The date sticks in my memory because it was the Halloween that a gang of us wrestled a huge horse-drawn four-wheeled flatbed conveyance once used to haul logs to the local mills onto the roof of the state forestry building near the corner of Cloquet Avenue and Eighteenth Street. The rig stayed up there for several days while most of the community passed by to see the engineering marvel. The forestry people finally had to borrow a crane from the match factory across the street to get it down.

Our new address was 1805½ Carlton Avenue—the ½ signifying it was the small house behind the main house fronting the street. The place was generally referred to as Gunnard Johnson's shack.

The house was tiny—a living room (where I slept on a studio couch), a kitchen with a wood-fired range and a sink (Mom cooked on a three-burner kerosene stove placed atop the range in the heat of the summer), a small bedroom with a curtain for a door, and a minute cubbyhole with a flush toilet so cramped into the limited space that a user had to decide how to approach it (face forward or backside to) well in advance. Bathing was done in a galvanized washtub in front of the range or, occasionally, at one of several public saunas. Stuccoed on the exterior with gray cement, the building was tight enough to handle the severest Minnesota winter with heat from the wood-burning range.

Keeping the stove going was my responsibility. We ordered wood by the cord, usually tamarack, which was unceremoniously dumped in a heap in our yard. When it arrived, I had two choices: pile it in our half of Johnson's garage as delivered and then split enough from day to day to meet our needs or chop and stack the entire load in one day of ax-swinging frenzy and get it over with.

I don't remember anyone ever teaching me to use an ax, but I'm sure my father didn't turn me loose with one without instruction.

116

I did destroy a good pair of boots once but fortunately missed my foot by millimeters. I had a lot more respect for the dangers involved after that.

Taking out the ashes was my job, too. I sprinkled some on the driveway in winter for traction purposes and spread the rest in the alley next to the garage. Spring runoff carried them down the hill toward the Lost Tavern and the match factory to be seen no more.

I liked living in Gunnard Johnson's shack. Dad had his steady job at the paper mill, we ate well, and the winter in Texas seemed to have broken my siege with illnesses. Another plus was that a lot of kids my age lived in the neighborhood, some of whom remained my lifelong friends. It was also the neighborhood where I became aware of her—my first consuming, passionate love, but that was still about two years down the road.

18

Potpourri

Moving to the house on Cloquet Avenue and then to Johnson's shack meant I had to switch from Jefferson Elementary to Garfield Elementary School where I was assigned to Miss Aili Siltanen's sixth grade class.

My first buddy at Garfield Elementary was Bob Sundeen. We knew each other from having suffered together through Miss Olive Park's fourth grade at Jefferson Elementary. And I mean suffered. If that female ever had a happy day, we never saw it. As my father told my mother once, not realizing I was within earshot, "The only thing wrong with that woman is her cherry's turned green with envy." I couldn't fathom what cherries had to do with Miss Park, but I filed the information away in my memory bank along with a thousand other things you'll understand when you get older.

Miss Park was continually coming down with a vengeance on some poor soul, mostly male, for petty infractions. One day, Miss Norman, the district's school nurse, made one of her routine visits, checking everyone for lice and peeking down throats. We'd open our mouths and gag "Ahh-hh-ugh" as she sighted along the tongue depressor at our innards. As she finished her inspection of each student, she'd deposit the wooden depressor into a wastebasket at her side.

I don't know how he finagled it, but Bob Sundeen managed to retain his tongue depressor, a big no-no. Bob's desk was in the outside row. During one of Miss Park's interminable lectures, the forbidden depressor got away from him and somersaulted in a high arc across the width of the room. All hell broke loose. Miss Park, fit to burst a blood vessel, jerked Bob out of his seat and shook him so he danced like a fresh-hanged cattle rustler on the end of a rope, all the while heaping vilifications on his little fourth grade head. I knew how he felt. In the third grade I purposely shoved a girl into a mud puddle on the playground. I don't recall why I did the dastardly deed, but I clearly remember my teacher, Miss Dolan, slapping me across the face with a roundhouse right that nearly took my head off and then slamming me into my seat. I didn't cry because as she stood there haranguing me for my transgression, the boy sitting behind me was patting me between the shoulder blades and whispering, "You done good!"

I don't know if we were just a bunch of hard-case dullards or what, but Miss Park devised a system of seating meant to shame us into more academic effort. The front seat on the left side of the room was assigned to the best student with each following desk, down one row and up the next, of decreasing value until the first desk in the last row belonged to the lowest achiever in the class. Supposedly, each grading period students would move forward or backward according to their successes or failures. It didn't work. We started out with most of the girls on the "bright" side of the room and most of the boys on the other. There was no place for more than one "best" which fostered great dissension among four or five girls vying for the top spot. Floyd Johnson, the lad relegated to the last seat, was defeated before the race started. His position labeled him as the class dunce. Miss Park might as well have tattooed a scarlet D on his forehead. He felt like a leper, his self-worth shattered. Floyd was a nice boy, very quiet and polite, but just wasn't a student. He held that desk until, finally, some parents objected to the system and it was stopped. (Floyd was killed fighting the Japanese in the Philippines during World War II.)

Every kid growing up with northern Minnesota winters learns early on that cold metal and warm, moist flesh are inseparable as a pair of dogs in a heat of passion. The lesson is usually learned in two steps: first, the child is told of the hazard, probably by an adult, and secondly, with the inherent skepticism of youth, he tests it out for himself. At least once every year that I attended Cloquet elementary schools, the school bell would summon the troops from recess leaving some experimenter behind with his tongue stuck to a piece of iron playground equipment. Release was accomplished by a teacher or a janitor with a teakettle full of hot water. I barely touched the tip of my tongue to an iron chinning bar support and left it when the bell rang. It took about a week for my body to regenerate the missing piece.

Most sixth grade boys at Garfield School served at least one grading period as crossing guards. Like postmen, we were out in all sorts of weather, stopping cars so our fellow students could cross the intersections safely. (If there was a momentary pause in the traffic, we'd hold everybody up until some came along.) The reward for being a school patrolman was free admission to the Saturday matinees at the Leb Theater. It was pretty heady stuff to be able to flash your badge and swagger into the movie while the peasants had to come up with a nickel.

I can only remember schools closing once because of the weather. Mr. E.B. Anderson, the superintendent, took education too seriously to let Mother Nature interfere. The day he relented, we all awoke to temperatures thirty-five degrees below zero and a fifty mile-per-hour wind. It was a Wednesday, and Wednesday afternoon was matinee time at the Leb Theater, a mid-week respite for housewives whose kids were in school and husbands off at work. It also happened that a movie starring the celluloid darling of the silver screen, the one and only Shirley Temple, was the presentation for the day.

When Mr. Anderson chanced to drive past the theater shortly after lunch, he nearly suffered a stroke. Every kid in town, icicles hanging from dripping noses, big siblings holding onto little ones so they wouldn't blow away, was lined up for a block waiting for the doors to open. Schools never closed again. Only once after that do I recall everybody being released early because of blizzard conditions, but that time the snow had almost drifted to St. Bernard and brandy proportions before we were let go.

Of course, winter had its rewards, and ice skating ranked high on the list. Every fall, Garfield School's open play area, the scene of soccer, football, and baseball games in season, was surrounded with two-inch by twelve-inch planks laid on edge and banked on the outside with earth. As soon as the average temperatures dropped below freezing, the enclosed playground was flooded, a warming house with a potbellied stove moved into place, and a few floodlights erected to illuminate the ice. A city employee policed the area, kept the fire going and reflooded the rink after shutdown each night about 10:00 P.M.

Most boys favored hard-toed hockey blades, while girls went for figure skates (Sonja Henie was the Queen of the Ice at the time). Not many boys actually played hockey, and not many girls fooled around with triple jumps and the like. Those feeling the urges of puberty spent their time skating as couples, while younger sprouts tore around the rink making nuisances of themselves.

Along toward the spring the 1938, the whole student body at Garfield took the Minnesota Seashore Musical Aptitude Test. It consisted mostly of listening to a note on the piano and then picking it out of a group played in a series. I was told my score was high but really didn't care one way or the other.

School always terminated for the summer the Wednesday preceding Memorial Day. The ink was hardly dry on my final sixth grade report card when a man showed up at our door informing my folks that they had a virtual musical genius on their hands. He insisted that a latent talent such as mine should not be wasted and suggested I take lessons on an instrument, a violin or the piano perhaps. My mother, of course, was thrilled. But all I could think of was Dudley Fuller.

Dudley Fuller was about my age and lived somewhere on the west side of town. When we resided on Tenth Street, Dudley would trudge by every Saturday carrying his violin along Cloquet Avenue going to and from his lessons on the east side of town. He never looked happy. In fact, he verged on belligerent. Dudley was a tough kid. He had to be. Every bully on the avenue hassled him coming and going because of the violin. It was even worse in summer when his mother made him wear short pants.

(I lost track of Dudley when we left Tenth Street and didn't see him again until our paths chanced to cross briefly at the U.S. Naval Training Center, Farragut, Idaho, early in 1944. Making conversation, I happened to mention his violin. He cursed steadily for a good five minutes without repeating himself. I never saw or heard of Dudley again, but I'll wager he didn't become a concert violinist.)

The man with the music test scores, pencil poised over his order pad, asked me which instrument I'd be interested in. I wasn't about to follow in Dudley Fuller's footsteps if I could help it. Grasping at straws, I came up with one that was affordable, small enough to fit into our tiny house, and could easily be hidden from skeptical view.

"The harmonica," I answered. We never saw that man again.

Because my birthday was always overshadowed by Christmas, my parents tried to make up for it by giving me a special gift in midsummer. When I was twelve, Dad presented me with a .22 caliber Model 67 bolt-action single-shot Winchester rifle. I'd hinted around for a Daisy air gun, but my father wouldn't hear of it. "BB guns are good for nothing but blinding people and breaking windows," summed up his opinion on the subject.

Firearms were not a novelty around our home. Mostly we owned rifles, but once, when we lived on Tenth Street, Dad brought home a Colt .45 automatic. I'm not certain where he got it but would guess he probably let somebody have a bottle of moonshine for it.

121

Having no real need for a hand gun, he removed the ammunition clip and gave the weapon to me. I was probably the only kid in Minnesota with a working .45 in his toy box. Dad finally sold the gun when we left for Texas several years later.

Being the proud owner of a .22 didn't mean I was turned loose with it. Dad wouldn't let the rifle out of the house unless he came with me. He taught me how to use and care for it, and we had many great hours together target shooting and hunting partridge. A favorite place for plinking was the city dump north of town. I eventually became proficient enough to hit bottles tossed into the air at least fifty percent of the time.

My father was not one to lavish praise, but I knew he was proud of my shooting ability, because he was willing to back it with hard cash.

Visiting Dad's boyhood friends in Crosby, Minnesota, on Labor Day weekend was an annual ritual while we lived in Cloquet. Dad and his buddies, mostly iron miners, would spend a few hours of the holiday celebrating in a neighborhood tavern while their womenfolk visited and kept an eye on the kids. The summer I got my .22 (c. 1937), the tavern in Crosby had put in a shooting gallery, an enclosed elongated box with a bulletproof backing and a pulley arrangement for placing the target and retrieving it. The target was a small card with a tiny, red "S" printed in each corner and one in the middle. The object was to completely obliterate an "S" with three rounds fired from a .22 rifle. Three shots cost twenty-five cents. A ten dollar bill was the prize for wiping out an "S."

Dad picked me up from my play and took me back to the tavern with him. No one had ever managed to collect the ten-dollar prize, and most of the people present didn't think it could be done. Dad covered a number of side bets, paid the barkeep twenty-five cents and handed me the weapon. My father's faith in my marksmanship unnerved me a little, especially when he'd backed up his conviction with hard-earned money. Because of the relatively short distance from the shooter's position to the target, Dad advised me to take a fine bead. The rifle had a pump action. Once I'd started, I fired the three allotted rounds in rapid succession.

"My God, he did it!" someone exclaimed.

The bartender retrieved the target and took it into the sunlight by the window. "Well . . . , it's close," he mumbled.

"Close, hell!" another tavern patron objected. "You owe the kid a sawbuck!" Others agreed.

Not only did I collect the ten spot, I got to keep all of it. By Minnesota law, I could be in the tavern, but I wasn't allowed to buy a round for the house to toast my good fortune.

I think Dad picked up enough on side bets to more than cover what he'd spent on my Winchester.

My father didn't believe in killing anything unless it could be eaten. Once on a partridge hunt, I shot a squirrel. Dad wasn't happy about it. The deed was done, however, so I removed the animal's beautiful tail and attached it to my hunting cap. In life, that squirrel had hosted at least a million fleas; in death, it got its revenge by giving them all to me! By the time we reached home those vermin were racing up and down my body inside my long-handled underwear, biting out great chunks of my flesh at random. My cap, the squirrel's tail still attached, went into the fiery bowels of our stove. The rest of my clothes were salvaged by being cooked in a copper boiler (whites— sheets, pillowcases, underwear—weren't judged clean unless boiled in a copper tub in those days). I itched and scratched for a week.

There must be an inviolable natural law that says a boy's Saturdays must be intruded upon by some irritating, day-ruining obligation. Whereas Dudley Miller had his violin lessons, I had the church bulletins.

We were members of Our Savior's Lutheran Church (also known as the Norwegian Lutheran Church) on the corner of Carlton Avenue and Eighth Street. "We" meaning my mother and me—my father usually worked on Sundays, much to his relief. The church's pastor insisted that every member of the congregation receive a church bulletin and weekly newsletter on Saturday, perhaps hoping to reel in a few backsliders to the Sunday sermon or, more deviously, trying to keep some of the boys out of the sinful billiards room at the Civic Center. My mother had proffered my services as a delivery boy. I objected strenuously, of course, but it was wasted breath.

I wasn't alone. There were about a dozen of us, all coerced, to cover the routes blanketing the community. We moaned and complained, but we did the job (it took a couple of hours at most). Then, in the summer of 1938, we were rewarded with a two-day trip to the Twin Cities. Some of the group had never been ten miles out of Cloquet; a few had been as far away as Duluth, about twenty miles. A couple of the boys backed out at the last minute because we were going "too far."

We traveled in three cars (five boys and a driver in each), and the first day we toured the capitol building in St. Paul and visited a candy and cookie factory in Minneapolis. Reverend Rossing, one of the three adults accompanying us aged considerably with each passing minute. He couldn't keep us together. At the capitol we scattered like young horses let out to pasture for the first time, racing through the marbled corridors, sliding down polished banisters and yoo-hooing to hear the echoes bounce wildly in the cavernous rotunda. At the candy and cookie factory, cookies of countless varieties were moving down different conveyor belts where apron-clad ladies with hair nets on their heads were boxing them and tossing rejects into discard bins. A bit awed, we hesitated until a woman motioned to the broken heaps of cookies and said, "Help yourselves." In an instant we were spread out like BB's from a shotgun blast, stuffing our faces and pockets with our particular favorites. Reverend Rossing's glasses fogged with anxiety-produced perspiration. In a state of shock at our hogs-at-the-trough behavior, he finally managed to bunch us up and move the group toward the exit when he discovered that Art Henderson was missing. "Where is Arthur?" he implored, an audible tightness in his throat.

"We'll find him!" we shouted and again scattered in all directions like mercury from a shattered thermometer. Moving like a pillaging raiding party through the factory, we searched every nook and cranny, helping ourselves to sweets along the way. Art was finally located in a distant warehouse section of the plant. He was sitting on the floor alongside a loosely packed, paper-lined crate of orange and black jellybeans, busily fishing the black ones out from between the slats.

We spent the night at church-affiliated St. Olaf College in Northfield, Minnesota. The institution was more or less closed for the summer, but we were housed in an empty women's dormitory, four boys to a room containing two three-quarter size beds. I was assigned to share a bed with Art Henderson. Nighty-night prayers were intoned by the reverend, lights were extinguished and silence descended on the hallowed halls, interrupted only by quiet, measured breathing. Peace. Then, Art slipped out of bed, taking our blanket with him. I waited expectantly in the dark. Soon a wailing, high-pitched falsetto voice echoed eerily through the hushed building. "Ooo-oo-o, I'm the ghost of St. Olaf," cried the spirit, a barefoot poltergeist shrouded in a gray cotton blanket. Lights flashed on down the hall. The ghost of St. Olaf, bare feet slapping on the linoleum-tiled floors, pounded into our room and hit the bed like a truckload of rocks dropping into a ditch. Our room light snapped on to reveal the reverend, clad in a calf-length nightshirt and breathing hard, holding our blanket. Blinking accusingly at Art who was snoring up a gale, he threw the blanket at us, muttered something under his breath, snapped off the light, and left. A *fait accompli* . . . the preacher had cussed!

We must have slept some. Up early, we rinsed the cockroaches and earwigs out of the sinks in the gang toilet, splashed a little water on our faces and breakfasted in Northfield's bank-turned-restaurant famous for an 1876 shoot-out between the James-Younger gang and Northfield's citizens. (Frank and Jesse James escaped. Three others—Clell Miller, Charlie Pitts, and Bill Chadwell—were shot to death. The three Younger brothers, Cole, Jim, and Bob, were given life sentences in the Minnesota State Penitentiary.)

Our last stop before commencing the long ride home was the reformatory in St. Cloud, Minnesota, probably to counterbalance the breakfast tainted with the spirits of Frank and Jesse. I was impressed with the massive, forbidding walls, the armed guards watching from every vantage point, the long rows of tiered cells with small name plates beside each barred door stating the occupant's crime—most in the section we visited said "manslaughter." The tour ended with a lecture by a prison administrator advising us to behave ourselves, obey the law and not return as inmates. We were a quiet group when we filed out of the prison.

Mention of our journey was made from the pulpit in Cloquet the Sunday after our return. The trip was extolled as a rewarding learning experience and a just compensation for our faithful service to God and the church.

I don't believe the trip was ever repeated.

19

Back to Texas and a Murder

The first day in the seventh grade was a traumatic experience for many of my classmates. Most had attended the same elementary school from kindergarten through the sixth grade, and the move to the junior-senior high school on Carlton Avenue between Fifth and Sixth Streets was a bit like taking up residence in a foreign country. For the first couple of days, they moved about the building in tight little security packs, all trying to stand on the same spot at the same time. It being my fifth school change, I couldn't get too excited.

On entering Miss Anna Tuttle's homeroom, I ran into a familiar face from the old Tenth Street neighborhood. Scotty Mattson was three or four years older than I and had been something of a permanent fixture in a couple of his elementary grades. Now he was beginning his third year in the seventh grade at the same desk—front seat, first row—under the stern, inhibiting eyes of Miss Tuttle. I don't recall Scotty ever causing Miss Tuttle any problems. He just sat quietly and let education flow around him like river water around a sturdy rock. When I entered the eighth grade the next year, he was gone. Having reached sixteen, he was not required under the laws of the sovereign State of Minnesota to return and so didn't. Scotty, a muscular boy with the shape and seemingly the constitution of a brick, eventually had a career as a fireman with the Cloquet Fire Department. Married and raising a family, it was a shock to the community when, while still a relatively young man, Scotty died of a sudden heart attack.

Miss Tuttle taught English, but I didn't learn much of it. She was a strict disciplinarian who tolerated no nonsense and saw no place for even a tiny bit of levity in the course of carrying out her task. As a result, I spent most of my hour in her class each day watching the big clock on the wall, urging the hands to move faster. I'm afraid it

126

would have been an interminably long year for both of us, but as it happened, we didn't have to find out.

The winter in Texas (1936-1937) had done wonders for my health, allowing me to breeze through the next Minnesota winter in good order. My folks and I had convinced ourselves that I was out of the woods physically when, in November 1938, I was again laid low with a massive mastoid-sinusitis infection. The doctors, in light of my previous recovery, suggested we repeat the treatment before my whole body was again run down. My father didn't hesitate. He had the 1932 Chevy serviced and my mother and Jeanette Angell, a recent high school graduate and the daughter of one of my mother's friends from the Norwegian Lutheran Ladies' Aid, and I headed south. It was hard for my folks to split the family again, but they both knew there was no work in Texas for my father.

Although it was only early November, there was already a fair amount of snow on the ground in northern Minnesota. By the time we reached Iowa, however, the white stuff was behind us. A couple of days out of Cloquet, we spent the night at a motel (a cluster of "tourist cabins," they were called tourist courts in those days) in Atoka, Oklahoma. Getting an early start in the morning, we had just cleared Atoka's southern city limit when our car developed a loud, insistent knock in its engine. Mom pulled off to the side of the road and shut the machine down.

A man in a dilapidated truck going toward the town stopped and asked if he could help. My mother said we needed a mechanic, and he promised to send someone to the rescue. While we waited in the frosty dawn, a teen-aged boy emerged from a crumbling log cabin across the road from where we were parked and ambled slowly up to our car. "Broke down?" he asked. Learning that we were and that help was supposedly on the way, he added, "Ma says y'all can come set by the fire if y'like." The morning was cool, one of those where the air is so still and crisp that smoke lazes straight up from the chimneys. Before we could take the boy up on his offer, however, an ancient flatbed truck with the words AL'S GARAGE, ATOKA, OKLA., painted on its ill-fitting doors rattled onto the scene. Al, proprietor of Al's Garage, had my mother fire up the engine. He listened to the ominous pounding for a scant moment and said, "Turn her off. Y'all got a busted rod."

Al towed us to his ramshackle business and, with the help of another man, spent most of the day putting the Chevrolet in order. Killing time, Mom and Jeanette wandered through the stores of

Atoka while I opted to hang around the garage, with Al's permission, and pretended to understand what was going on. In the afternoon, bored with waiting, I wandered into the vacant lot behind Al's place. I was sitting on an old tire, soaking up the fall Oklahoma sunshine when a girl appeared out of nowhere. One minute I was alone and the next this girl was sharing my tire. "My name's Betty Jo Jones," she said. "What's yourn?" She was maybe a couple of years younger than me. "Where y'all from?" she wanted to know.

I told her.

"Never heered tell of it," she admitted.

We had nothing in common. The conversation lagged. Betty Jo opened a much-traveled, once-white paper bag she was carrying. "Y'all want some of my candy?" I looked into the sack. It was about a third full of very tired hard rock candy fused into a single lump. I graciously declined.

A female voice from a nearby house intruded. "Betty Jo, git yourself in here right now! Gran'ma's waitin' on you."

Betty Jo kicked our tire and skipped away in the direction of the command. "See y'all agin sometime," she called over her shoulder.

"Sure, sometime," I agreed. Of course, we never met again.

The car was ready by late afternoon. Mom had been worried about what it was going to cost; two women and a boy stranded far from home were pretty much at the mechanic's mercy. The final bill, however, was much lower than she had expected. Hardly more than the cost of parts. Mom paid cash, which surprised Al. Apparently most of his labor during the Depression years was paid for on "a little now and the rest when you can catch me" basis.

Looking back across a span of nearly sixty years, I'm impressed with the generosity of those we met in Oklahoma. Thinking of them now, I'm reminded of a bindle stiff, an old ex-Wobbly I once chanced to meet. "If you ever need help or a hand-out," he advised, "stay away from the ritzy side of town. They'll just sic their dogs on you. Go to those with little to spare. They'll always do their best."

Besides the poverty and the friendliness of the people, two other things stand out in my mind whenever I hear the name Oklahoma: turtles and locusts. Highballing across the state on one of our several journeys, we came to about a twenty-mile stretch of highway that was literally crawling with high-backed box turtles, all moving in the same direction. There were thousands of them, part of a mass migration of some kind. We tried not to hit any of them, but it was virtually impossible. They knew where they were going, too. When we stopped to watch, I tried to point several of them in another direction, but they would have none of it—a mass of a single mind.

Early one morning in another part of the state, we stopped for gasoline at an out-of-the-way station to find the attendant digging out his single service bay with a Minnesota-style snow shovel. Instead of white powder, however, he was removing large piles of dead, brown locusts, some three to four inches long. They had passed through during the night, a blizzard of giant insects smashing into unseen obstacles and dying in drifted heaps.

Instead of continuing south from Dallas-Fort Worth, we turned toward the vast, lonely stretches of west Texas. Al of Al's Garage had told Mom he'd heard a rumor that big things were happening in Odessa, Texas, that there were jobs to be had in the oil fields. She decided to check it out, hoping there would be something for my father. Although Odessa did see an oil boom some years later, the rumor turned out to be just that—a rumor. At the time of our visit, Odessa was a windblown, dusty pimple of civilization with no visible reasons for being.

The trip across West Texas was lonely, hot and dry. On one stretch, we covered 109 miles between communities and saw maybe four other vehicles in the whole distance. It was near the end of one of those desolate runs that the Chevrolet balked again. Fingers crossed, we limped into what had to be the smallest hamlet in Texas. I don't recall its name if, in truth, it had one. It consisted of a single gasoline pump, a dilapidated, sandblasted clapboard building posing as a garage, and one faded, reddish-brown railroad boxcar sitting off on a rusty railed siding. The boxcar, its doors wide open in the hope of catching some air, was obviously the home of a large Mexican family. Numerous souls of all conceivable ages lolled in the boxcar's shade or busied themselves with household chores, cooking on an open fire and washing clothes in a bucket.

It was nothing short of a miracle, but the garage's operator, the only Anglo evident in the community, had a replacement fuel pump to fix the Chevy. As he worked on the car, my mother, observing there was no sign of a food source in any direction on the flat desert, asked how the Mexican family survived. "Six days a week they eat beans and jackrabbits," he answered. "On Sunday they have jackrabbits and beans." His tone of voice and general demeanor intimated he felt nothing but contempt for his neighbors.

129

Mom checked out the employment situation in El Paso, found nothing and decided to continue on to San Antonio. The journey southeastward was another long, weary haul through desert sands and cactus. The only break in the monotony came in the form of a broken fan belt. Digging into one of her suitcases, Mom brought out a rayon stocking (nylon wasn't yet available and silk too expensive for ordinary folks), wrapped it as tightly as she could around the fan belt pulleys and drove it for many miles until we located a regular replacement. The motor heated some but not to the point of boiling over.

Beautiful San Antonio! Palm trees, the meandering San Antonio River, Brackenridge Park, the Alamo, warm, sunshiny days. Yee haw!

We drove directly to West Sayer Street. Nothing had changed. The street was still a series of potholes dusted with gravel, Mr. Lonnie Curtis still sat in the sun in front of his tiny, two-pump gasoline station on the corner of Pleasanton Road and West Sayer, and Gray's Feed Store occupied its same position cater-corner from the gasoline station.

Mr. Curtis informed us that our old shack was occupied, but he thought the lady who owned the place directly across the street from it would be willing to rent. She was.

Our new home was really one end of what had been a Texas dog run—an elongated series of teetering buildings originally connected by breezeways but later boarded up and used for chicken coops, storage rooms, and a stable converted to a one-car garage. Mom and I slept on a screened-in porch with a rusty corrugated metal roof, while Jeanette Angell occupied a small room separated from us by a combination kitchen and living room. The john was located down the path just beyond a wire-enclosed chicken yard.

Settling in, the next day I was packed off to Harlandale Junior-Senior High School. Surprisingly, I met only one student I'd known in the fifth grade. I have no idea what became of the others, but populations of our economic level in Texas in the 1930s had to be highly transient to survive. Academically, I mostly repeated in the Texas seventh grade what I'd already had in the Minnesota sixth, but the day-to-day life experiences that came my way tended to balance it all out, one of the unscheduled lessons I could have done without.

It was unusually hot, one of those days when the kids without shoes hurried from shade to shade to keep from burning their feet. I was alone, walking home from school along a quiet residential street when the calm of the balmy afternoon was shattered by six very loud, rapid gunshots. I stopped dead in my tracks when the first one

130

went off, looking wildly about for the source. On the fourth blast, the front door of the house fifty feet in front of me on my side of the street slammed open. A woman crossed the porch in two running strides. Two more explosions went off behind her as she reached the outer edge of the platform. Her legs twisted awkwardly beneath her. She pitched face first down the four steps leading to the walkway to the street, rolled to her left onto the lawn, and came to rest on her back, arms outstretched on either side and one leg folded under her.

I couldn't see another human being anywhere. Nothing moved. Complete silence. I walked gingerly over to the woman. She was still, her open, glassy-blue eyes staring up into the sun. Blood soaked the front of her dress. More blood lay in congealing streaks from the corners of her mouth into her ears and her mussed, lightly-waved strawberry blonde hair. As I stood there wondering what to do, police cars, lots of them, sirens screaming, poured in from both ends of the street. Men in blue uniforms and others in ordinary business suits, weapons drawn, surrounded the house. One of them yelled, "Hey, you! Kid! Get the hell behind a tree!" I hunkered down in Saturday matinee cowboy fashion and scooted for the nearest sapling. I was back on Tenth Street in Cloquet but without my rubber gun!

The police called for whoever was inside the house to come out. Nothing happened. A man in civilian clothes, possibly a neighbor, arrived with a yarn-tied patchwork quilt and tossed it over the woman's body. Two detectives, hammers on their revolvers pulled back, bodies bent low, charged through the open doorway into the building.

By this time, at least three ambulances, a hearse, and fifty or so ambulance chasers had clogged the street, parking their cars on lawns, sidewalks, wherever. Finally, the two detectives emerged from the house with another man between them.

The prisoner seemed to be clutching something to his body with both hands as he was walked to one of the ambulances. I eased out from behind my tree and moved in close to see. The man's shirt was open and he was holding his intestines, which were bulging from a side to side slash across his abdomen. He stood there at the back of the ambulance, blood and viscera oozing between his fingers, talking to the police as the woman's body was loaded into the hearse. Then, he climbed into the ambulance with the two detectives.

Sweating and cursing, the police set about untangling the traffic jam, imploring everyone to clear the street and get on about their own business. A small white-and-black puppy with curly, woolly fur and bright, dark eyes wandered behind the rear wheel of a backing car. I screamed at the driver, but it was too late. The puppy's head was crushed flat. The driver climbed out of the auto, picked the still form up by one hind leg and tossed it under a hedge. Shrugging his shoulders at me as if to say, "That's life," he climbed back into his car and continued working his way through the traffic. At that moment, in a flash of insight, I came to realize that be it man's or beast's, life is a very temporary condition. It can end in unexpected seconds, and the body that's left is just . . . garbage.

I arrived home with tears in my eyes. Mom asked what was wrong. I told her a puppy had been run over and killed.

The next morning the front page of the *San Antonio Light* newspaper was devoted to the shooting. According to the report, the woman was killed by her husband who had recently been released from a mental institution. Using all of his ammunition on his wife, the man had then attempted suicide by slicing open his abdomen with two kitchen knives, breaking one in the process. He had died in the hospital that same night.

Realizing that I could have been on my way home from school when it happened, my mother asked if I'd seen anything. "Oh, yeah," I answered. "That's where the puppy got killed."

20

Prayers and Preyers

It was during our second winter in San Antonio that my vague suspicions about organized religions began to solidify into rock-hard conclusions.

My mother, of course, was still suffering me unto the house of the Lord, ever hopeful that I'd see at least a glimmer of the light. Unable to find a Norwegian Lutheran Church in the city, Mom sporadically dragged me off to one of the Missouri Synod models. The only difference between the Norwegian and Missouri factions as far as I could see, was that the Missouri bunch had a bowling alley in their Sunday school basement which, I'm certain, would have been considered an abomination in our Minnesota church like most fun things—except, of course, the annual lutefisk supper.

That winter of 1938-1939, I attended my one and only tent meeting held under a regular circus-type big top. I assume we never had the like in Cloquet because of the surfeit of churches already vying for the sinners' tithes. Anyway, word was circulated among the West Sayer Street populace that miracles were being performed nightly at a revival taking place on the east side of the city. People were being saved, the sick and maimed cured. Having done a lot of praying for my brother and me, Mom was skeptical of healing preachers, but she decided we'd attend for recreational purposes if nothing else. I balked. Mom sweetened the pot. There was, she said, going to be a famous lady there, and we might as well take in the free show. The only famous lady I'd ever seen was Sally Rand. That having been painless, I quit arguing.

The big tent was packed. Hundreds of people sat row upon row on tiered risers like chickens roosting in a coop and, as it turned out, waiting to be plucked. A stage had been erected at the back of the tent, flanked on one side by a fair-sized orchestra and on the other by a lusty-lunged choir. The ringmaster-preacher in charge ran the operation from stage right behind a lectern bristling with microphones.

The show began with soul-stirring hallelujah renditions by the choir and its accompanying orchestra. When the singers finally stopped to catch their breaths, the master of ceremonies got right down to business. People suffering from mental or physical infirmities or those concerned for anyone so afflicted were instructed to write the name of the heavily ladened on a slip of paper (readily available from a horde of assistants roaming the aisles) and deposit it along with a one dollar bill into the box provided on stage front. The orchestra played and the choir sang, while the sick and troubled queued up with their slips of paper and their dollars. When the last of the long line of supplicants had made their contributions, the ring manager made an appeal to the audience to support the church's radio messages to the shut-ins and to enrich the building fund for the new tabernacle being constructed on the site—"a rock of salvation, a monument to the Son of God and His great works." (We had noted a partial skeleton of steel I-beams dominating the sky behind the tent on our arrival.) The M.C. didn't leave it up to the donors to decide how much they wanted to give. He pitched, "We need thirty twenty dollar bills to maintain our Sunday school program," and the choir sang "Bringing in the Sheaves" over and over again until he got them. Then, it was fifty tens followed by forty fives and, finally, a hundred ones for this or that program while the choir droned on with their harvesting. The man got everything he asked for. The believers lined up, some with tears streaming as they parted with their rent and grocery money.

While all that cash flowed down the aisles to the stage, I wondered about that box full of names and dollar bills. I was getting butt weary from sitting on the hard risers, bored with the sheaf bringer-inners and had visions of having to sit through a long session as each donor was prayed for. My fears were unfounded. Having picked every available pocket in the tent, the ringmaster stood over the box, spread his arms wide, looked piously up toward the heavens, intoned, "The Lord knows who these needy souls are," mumbled a short prayer for the lot and nodded to an assistant who whisked the boodle away.

A few more preliminaries and the real show began. The big top was plunged into darkness. The crows waited in hushed expectation. The drums started a slow roll, building to an ear-shattering crescendo. Klieg lights suddenly flooded center stage and there she stood in a flowing robe of white, an angel out of a Sunday school pamphlet crowned with a cascade of glistening red hair, arms upraised to the heavens—the one and only Aimee Semple McPherson!

Miss McPherson, founder of the Foursquare Gospel Church, whose members in Cloquet were known as the Holy Rollers, exhorted us with her divine revelation of the four basic tenets of her belief: Regeneration, Divine Healing, the Second Coming of Christ, and the Baptism of the Holy Ghost. Her stage presence, the use of klieg lights, her shimmering hair, and the snow-white purity of her wrap, mesmerized many of the uncertain into becoming the true believers they really wanted to be when they entered the tent in the first place.

When Miss McPherson completed her part of the program, I figured that was it. But, no. The ringmaster again took over. Winding up the choir and the musicians, everybody joined in bringing in more of those damned sheaves while three-gallon buckets in lieu of collection plates were circulated through the crowd to pick up any loose change that might be left. As I watched those buckets get heavy with coins, I recalled an old Sunday school lesson. The money changers may have been cast out of the temple, but they weren't doing badly in a tent!

I was only thirteen years old when I saw Aimee Semple McPherson, but I readily pegged her as a ham with a scam and, as it came to pass, a pathfinder for latter-day Bible bangers: Robinson, Falwell, Swaggart, Bakker.

Cloquet had its share of Eagles, Masons, Knights of Columbus, and odd fellows without capital letters, but one Sunday in San Antonio, we came across a group I'd never heard of before—the Ku Klux Klan. We were looking for a place to have our picnic lunch, when we chanced upon a park-like setting complete with outdoor tables. We had barely settled in, wondering why no one else seemed to be using the place, when a man, obviously a caretaker, appeared and informed us that we were on private property. His intent was to send us on our way.

My mother, not one to be intimidated, wanted to know whose private property. The caretaker replied with a hint of menace that we were on Klan land and better be on our way. I was ignorant of the organization, but my mother wasn't, and she said later, "No simpleton who runs around in bed sheets and a dunce cap crowds me!" Hackles up, Mom let it be known that she had food on the table and wasn't going anywhere until we had eaten. If the Klan didn't want people using the place, they better put up a sign or build a fence.

On his own, in the face of righteous Danish indignation, the man became apologetic and actually invited us to stay. Noting that we had a small bellows-type Kodak, he did ask us not to take pictures. If I ever, heaven forbid, decide to run for public office, I suppose I'll have to burn the snapshot of me standing in front of a large, corrugated metal building with a sign over its entryway proclaiming in blazoned red letters:

✝

San Antonio
Ku Klux Klan No. 31

A real Christian group—you could tell by the cross. . . .

21

Mr. Curtis and Mr. Gray

Tending the sick was a very natural thing for my mother. She was good at it. As a young girl on the farm in Wisconsin, her father never considered bringing in a doctor if his wife or children were sick (he wasn't adverse, however, to sending for the veterinarian if one of the cows was in trouble). As a result, Mom picked up a fair amount of nursing skills watching and helping her mother get the family through the normal medical crises that are part of raising children. She also developed a tolerance for the sight of blood and viscera in the process of pulling birthing calves with her dad. Later, trying to keep me alive, she honed her talents to a near professional level. Mom could give shots, administer enemas, and dispense pills with the best of them, but probably more important, she had compassion for the ill and didn't hesitate if someone needed help. Such was the case with our Sayer Street neighbor Lonnie Curtis.

Mr. Curtis, originally from Illinois, had moved to Texas searching relief from chronic, severe asthma. He had been a long-haul truck driver but was forced to give it up because of his health problem. To support his wife and two daughters, he ran a tiny, two-pump gasoline station on the corner of West Sayer Street and Pleasanton Road, a couple of doors from his home. His was not a thriving business; if he netted two dollars a day, I'd be surprised.

I never saw Mr. Curtis dressed in anything but khaki. His shirts were the kind with big, button-down breast pockets, and those pockets bulged. On one side he kept his pipe tobacco pouch and on the other a bottle of adrenalin and a hypodermic syringe. He spent a lot of time sitting on a chair in front of his place of business, contemplating the world as it inched slowly and sporadically past his door. My friend Vernon Gaulley, about a year younger than my twelve, and I spent a fair amount of time sitting with Mr. Curtis. We had our reasons, but contemplating the world was not one of them. What really attracted us was the chance to watch him turn blue.

Mr. Curtis hated taking his adrenalin so would delay administrating it to himself as long as possible. In the throes of an asthma attack, he could inhale but then couldn't exhale. Attacks began with Mr. Curtis obviously unable to release his breath. He'd purse his lips and force the air out of his lungs as if he were blowing up an extra-stout balloon. Soon his face would get red, and he'd start fumbling in his shirt pocket for the bottle of adrenalin and his syringe. He'd struggle to unbutton his shirt cuff and push up the sleeve as his face began to darken. Finally, he'd manage to insert the needle into the bottle, draw out a measured dosage and push it into his thin, puncture-scarred arm. His face would turn blue-black, his eyes roll back in his head, and he'd lapse into unconsciousness with the spent syringe still dangling from his limp arm. About the time Vernon and I were sure he was dead, Mr. Curtis would commence breathing, his face and neck gradually turning from blue-black to pink to white, his eyes coming back into alignment, and then he'd be okay again for a couple of hours.

During our first winter in San Antonio, Mr. Curtis was in bad shape; when we returned the second time, he was much worse. Casting about for some relief, he would try anything—faith healers, herbalists, regular physicians, sleeping with a hairless Chihuahua at the foot of the bed, anything. Then someone told him about a new allergist in town.

The allergist, a regular medical doctor, had Mr. Curtis remove everything from his bedroom except a nonallergenic pad of some kind to sleep on and prescribed a regimen of hypodermically administered narcotics to keep him completely sedated for several days, a procedure that was supposed to break his adrenalin dependency and return his body to a normal chemical balance after which the doctor planned to zero in on what substance or substances in the environment were triggering his asthmatic attacks. It was a process normally handled in a hospital, but Mr. Curtis couldn't afford the luxury. He also couldn't afford a nurse to administer the drugs, keep distilled water running into his veins or take care of his other needs. Mrs. Curtis was one of those nice, personable folks who became faint just thinking about injections, defecations, and the like, so my mother volunteered to help. Mrs. Curtis followed one step behind Mom all through the episode, her hands fluttering uselessly like the wings of a baby sparrow who has left the nest too early. She was so busy trying to fly, she couldn't pick up a bedpan.

Doped out of his skull, Mr. Curtis didn't have any asthma attacks; but when the drugs were withdrawn, he relapsed immediately and went back on adrenalin to live. Then, he heard about a new chiropractic clinic and made an appointment.

At his initial screening, the spine aligners told him that after his next appointment he could throw away his adrenalin forever; they assured Mr. Curtis they would have him on his way to complete recovery with his first treatment.

Mrs. Curtis had never learned to drive an automobile, and her husband was in no shape to do it, so Mom drove them (in Texanese, she "carried" them) to the clinic. Mr. Curtis left his adrenalin and hypodermic syringe in the car with my mother while he and his wife went into the chiropractic offices. Mom was waiting patiently in the Chevrolet when three white-jacketed knuckle-poppers burst from the building. One had a hold of Mr. Curtis's legs while the other two gripped his arms. Mrs. Curtis, fluttering uselessly, brought up the rear. Red-faced and puffing from their efforts, the chiropractors dumped Mr. Curtis, his face blue-black, his eyes rolled back into his head, onto the Chevy's backseat, mumbled something about not wanting to see him again, and fled back to their clinic. Unruffled, my mother shoved some adrenalin into Mr. Curtis, and he returned to the living.

Mr. Curtis never did say what he thought when, on opening his eyes, he was confronted by two women, one fluttering and sobbing and the other holding her stomach and laughing hysterically.

Mr. Curtis never got better. A couple of years later, my mother received a letter from Mrs. Curtis saying he had died. His heart had given out from the years of strain put on it.

Mr. Gray, the owner of the feed store cater-corner from Curtis's gasoline station on Pleasanton Road, was also a sick man. I thought his name was a really fitting one. His complexion was gray, battleship gray. He had a Coca-Cola and aspirin habit. Everyday at precise two-hour intervals, Mr. Gray crossed the road from his place of business, purchased a six-ounce bottle of Coke from Mr. Curtis, and popped two aspirins. His hands always trembled as he fished the white tablets from their little metal box. According to Mr. Curtis, Mr. Gray had done this for years.

Vernon and I liked Mr. Gray. He let us pick green, unroasted peanuts out of his bales of peanut hay. He wasn't very communicative, though. We never learned where he lived or if he had a family. I do know his business wasn't doing any better than Mr. Curtis'.

When Mrs. Curtis wrote about her husband's demise, she mentioned that, after all those years, Mr. Gray had kicked his Coca-Cola and aspirin addiction. Mr. Gray, it seems, wasn't gray anymore.

22

Pets

Animals have always been a part of my life. I grew up with a long series of dogs, cats, a few goldfish, and one chameleon. (When my own children were growing up, we added a beer-drinking parakeet, a skunk, and a red-eared turtle that grew from the size of a dime to the dimension of a small dinner plate.)

Of the cats around in my early years, only one stands out sharply in my memory; a slate-gray tomcat aptly named Tommy. He was the hide-and-seek cat. During the many hours I spent convalescing alone in our house on Tenth Street while my folks worked at the Hotel Solem, Tommy and I played at the game. I'd hide, he'd find me. Then he'd hide, and I'd search for him. I don't know which of us enjoyed the game more, but he was the better at the contest. Of course, he had superior senses of smell and hearing, while my nose was chronically plugged and my ears stuffed with cotton.

Of dogs, there was an abundance. My folks had Buddy when I was born (he was the one that was poisoned in Michigan). Buddy was followed by a small black and white long-haired dog I know only from my baby pictures. Then came Midnight.

A black, basically shepherd with a tiny blaze of white on his chest and white feet, Midnight belonged to one of the guests at the Wright Hotel. He jumped into the truck when we moved to Tenth Street. We returned him to his master several times, but he wouldn't stay. Finally, his owner gave up and told us to keep him. Later, Midnight took up with my aunt Ida's husband, Henry Aho, and lived out his life with him. I really believe Midnight decided that because Henry caught so much hell at home for his drinking, the man needed a friend who'd accept his intemperance without censure.

Next in line was Skippy, a white terrier-type who was struck by a car on Cloquet Avenue. He made it down the hill to home and died in our yard just short of the front steps. Officer Ed Solem of the Cloquet Police Department, up in years and much overweight, loaded down with a Smith and Wesson Police .38, a belt full of bullets, handcuffs, Sam Browne belt, a billy, and a pair of large, heavy steel-toed, ankle-high shoes, wheezed onto the scene a couple of minutes behind the dog. Officer Solem prodded the lifeless animal with his billyclub and announced authoritatively, "He's dead." Without further comment, Officer Solem wiped the sweat from his face, squared his visored uniform hat and stomped heavily back up the hill toward Cloquet Avenue.

Jack, the bulldog left with my aunt Alena when we moved to Texas in 1936, was a mature dog when he was murdered by an unknown assailant. Alena found his bludgeoned body along the railroad tracks at the foot of Ninth Street. She blamed Parasol Jack, an ill-tempered character who passed through the neighborhood from time to time, but couldn't prove it. The two Jacks hated each other. Whenever they met, one growled while the other cursed.

Tippy, a small gray and white, short-haired dog with a doughnut tail curled up on his back, liked to climb the willow tree in our front yard between Fifteenth and Sixteenth Streets on Cloquet Avenue. Strangers driving through town often stopped to stare at the sight of a dog perched nonchalantly on a high limb, watching the traffic go by. In the end, he chased a ball into the street and was killed by a car. It was my fault. I'd been warned that it would happen if my friends and I insisted on playing where our ball could get away into the street. I didn't listen.

Cappy, a smooth-haired fox terrier, came to us in a trade of sorts. One Koski Marta's (Finnish reversal) daughter and her husband were just barely getting by on lower Eleventh Street when they were blessed with twins. The father was unemployed and without prospects. Food was scarce, they had other small children, and their situation was desperate. We had just moved into Gunnard Johnson's shack on Carlton Avenue when my mother was invited by Grandma Koski to see the twins. The babies, a boy and a girl, were laying naked in a cardboard box lined with old flour-sack dishtowels. The family lived in a tarpaper-covered shack that was an oven in the hot, humid summer weather. My mother, like every woman since Eve has done at the sight of newborns, even if they truly appeared to be perfect clones of Snowflake, the albino gorilla, took one look at the infants and exclaimed, "What beautiful babies!"

Grandma Koski, sitting on a box in the corner of the room, quietly sucking hot coffee through a cube of lump sugar, said flatly, "They can't keep them. They have to give them up."

The twins' mother, her face haggard from an apparent lack of sleep and the burden of the decision, wiped a tear from her cheek with the back of her hand and asked Mom in a whisper, "Will you take them, Alice?"

Mom was sorely tempted. She cried over the babies. They were malnourished, suffering from severe diaper rash, mosquito and bedbug bites, and other assorted inflammations. She and Dad talked it over. After agonizing most of the night, they decided reluctantly that they couldn't afford twins either (they were deeply in debt to the medical profession). Mom, however, was determined to do something about those babies. She called on one of her Ladies' Aid friends, a Mrs. Sondersen who lived in a large, comfortable home not far from Pinehurst Park on the west side of town. The Sondersens were middle-aged and childless. Mom took them to see the twins and then there were three women crying. The Sondersens had wanted children but weren't so blessed. Mrs. Sondersen wondered if her spoiled fox terrier, Cappy, would adjust. Mom took the dog, the Sondersens adopted the twins.

Cappy was a good one. He moved right in and claimed his share of my studio couch and half the back seat of the Chevy. He also decided he owned the neighborhood, although Rex, a water spaniel belonging to the Barr family up the street, didn't exactly agree. Rex did, however, grant Cappy domain on our side of Carlton Avenue. In the end, it was Cappy's eternal vigilance over his territorial claim that put him down. He loved to ride in the car, but like most people when they leave home, he must have worried about his unguarded dominion. On returning from a trip to the store or anywhere else, Cappy would leap out of the Chevy and dash madly back to the street, barking and raising a great fuss to let all real or imagined interlopers know that he was again on guard and they'd better shape up. At first he'd race just to the end of the driveway, then prance back with the air of one who has done his duty. But, like bordering states separated by a river, he decided that his property rights extended to mid-channel or the center line of Carlton Avenue. The inevitable consequence of his quirk was obvious. We tried to break him of it but failed. The driver of the car didn't have a prayer of avoiding the dog, but I still think the s.o.b. could have at least stopped and offered his condolences.

It was on West Sayer Street in San Antonio that Schultz came into our lives. He'd been branded a chicken killer and was scheduled to be destroyed for it. I don't remember where my mother learned about the animal, but we drove out to a small ranch (I'm being polite;

it was really a sand-blown hole of collapsed fences, slumping sheds, and rotting manure piles) to see the dog. He was a compact bundle of muscle, a Heinz, mostly fox terrier with a black-patched coat of white, short, bristle-like fur and a mere stub of a tail. He had one black ear and one white and his eyes sparked with mischief as if to ask, "Well now, who the hell are you?"

I wanted the dog as soon as I saw him, but Mom hesitated. He was, after all, an accused chicken killer, and the lady we rented from had chickens and let them run free during the daylight hours. "If y'all don't take him," said his whisker-stubbled owner, "I'm gonna shoot him." We took the dog.

Schultz, so christened by his original owner to worst a neighbor by the same name, bared his lack of social graces almost immediately. Minutes after we arrived home, he was hit by a car on Pleasanton Road. He rolled to his feet and chased the offender down the thoroughfare. A half-hour later, he was stepped on by a horse who got the same treatment as the auto. The horse squared away, Schultz tore all the flapping clothes on our washline to shreds. We tied him up for about a day and a half after the last episode. Finding himself tethered, the dog must have given his situation some serious thought. He never again chased cars or horses, nor did he bother the drying clothes. (When Mom wrote Dad about the new dog, she told him she'd been ready to kill Schultz that first day. He wrote back and said, "Better not. He sounds like family.")

It turned out that Schultz wasn't really an incorrigible chicken killer. He'd just been surviving as best he could. Once he learned that he would be fed regularly, he gave up chicken. He still loved to bunch them up, however, and then plow through the middle of the flock like a cannon-fired bowling ball, sending squawking hens and feathers in all directions.

I don't think Schultz considered himself a dog or a pet. He appointed himself titular head of our household and had a pet of his own—a cow. Neighbors down the road from us had a bony old Holstein they staked along the ditchbank to graze. Every day, Schultz would visit the cow and often the two of them would take a noontime siesta with the dog snoozing contentedly between the bovine's front legs.

We had Schultz for more than sixteen years. He developed heart trouble in his old age, maybe the result of demanding and receiving a cup of coffee laced heavily with cream and sugar every morning. (Mom would mutter, "Damned spoiled dog," as she fixed

Schultz's daily jolt, but it was she who got him started on the habit in the first place.) He took a little red "heart pill" along with his morning brew for years. Along the line, he also lost one eye in a fight. Its loss ultimately contributed to his death. He was chasing a canine trespasser out of his yard in Washington State when he ran under the wheels of a car approaching on his blind side. The driver was a neighbor and close friend. He felt as bad as we did.

My mother abhorred reptiles. The mere sight of a garter snake in her flower beds would send her packing.

We were living on Tenth Street in Cloquet when I sold a year's subscription to *The Open Road for Boys* magazine to a friend (never a salesman, I think it was the only thing I ever sold). In lieu of a cash commission, I opted for a chameleon. I don't remember why I wanted the creature, but its touted ability to change colors to match its surroundings probably had something to do with my choice.

We'd had the lizard around for a couple of days when Reynold Johnson asked if he could put it on display in his hardware store on Cloquet Avenue. My mother jumped at the opportunity to share a little herpetological culture with the rest of the citizens of Cloquet—any damn thing to get the critter out of her house. In about a week, however, the chameleon's novelty and customer draw at the store wore off, and we had him back.

To give the chameleon some freedom from his screened-over shoe box, I daily released him onto our living room window sill where he seemed content to wander on his own. One day I forgot to retrieve him, and he disappeared. Mom started suffering stress symptoms almost immediately. She'd wake up at night in cold sweats, dreaming "that thing" was going to walk across her face as she slept. I searched diligently, but the reptile had vanished. About two weeks elapsed. Mom was just beginning to feel that maybe the lizard had somehow escaped from the house and was gone for good. Then, one morning as she was dusting furniture, Mom went to move a framed picture sitting on an end table when the chameleon. blended unseen into the photo, leaped out at her. The picture flew one way, Mom went the other, and I caught the beast before he could disappear again.

Under strict orders, I bid good-bye to the chameleon and released him beneath the lilac bush in front of the house. I tried to tell my mother that he would freeze to death come winter, but, somehow, I got the impression she *really* didn't care.

145

23

Expanding Horizons

We left Texas in May 1939. I've never been back. There was no need. By the time I reached my teens, I'd already done battle with most of the bugs floating around and have rarely had so much as a cold since.

My folks allowed me a lot of slack as I was growing up. As long as I checked in and let them know where I was going, I pretty much had free rein. That was also true to varying degrees for all of my friends.

There were, of course, a few kids who had even more leeway than I did. Down the hill to the north of our shack on Carlton Avenue was an unmarked dead-end road (now called Avenue G) that ran east off Eighteenth Street. It was a short, graveled lane that ended in a kind of cul-de-sac with a handful of rundown houses bunched haphazardly around a beer joint appropriately named the Lost Tavern. Two of the families who lived there stand out in my memory because of their numbers and their lack of restraints.

The Karjala boys were probably Cloquet's most successful catfish harvesters. There were a number of them—they seemed to move in a small, homogeneous crowd—the oldest a year or two younger than myself. They spent their summers, night and day, unsupervised, angling for channel catfish in the St. Louis River. And they caught fish—real lunkers. It wasn't unusual to see a collection of Karjalas toting catfish longer than they were through the streets after a night along the river. Most Cloquet people shunned fish from the St. Louis River. Its waters carried raw sewage and industrial waste from every community along its length and dumped it into Lake Superior. The Karjalas, however, always appeared fit and sassy and had no qualms about eating their catches.

(After World War II, because of population increases and lowering water tables affecting the city's wells, water was piped into

Cloquet from Lake Superior some twenty miles to the east through a series of pumping stations, no small project considering the untold tons of slate rock that had to be dynamited in the process. I was visiting in Cloquet about the time the system was activated, and my uncle Swen summed up the feelings of many of the town's citizens when he said, "For eighty years we've been sending our shit down the river to Lake Superior. Now they're sending it back so we can drink it!")

At times, the easygoing attitudes some folks passed on to their kids could lead to the absurd. Another family living in the Lost Tavern cul-de-sac was the Stoddards. One of the boys was in some of my eighth grade classes. What I recall about him in particular is his right thumb; it was missing at the first knuckle. Of course, I had to ask what had happened it. "My brother and I were splitting firewood," he said. "Our mother yelled at us to be careful and not cut off our fingers. My brother looked at me and asked, 'I wonder what it would be like to cut off a finger?' I put my thumb on the chopping block and said, 'Find out.' Damned if he didn't."

From ages twelve through sixteen, my closest friends were Bobby Barr and Bob Sundeen. Throughout the summers, we covered the countryside on foot, bicycles, and by hitchhiking. Winters kept us a little closer to home.

One of our favorite summer destinations was Park Point (labeled Minnesota Point on road maps) in Duluth. We'd thumb rides the twenty miles to downtown Duluth and then walk to the Aerial Lift Bridge and out on the north jetty extending into Lake Superior from the city's harbor basin. We liked this trip because, in the heat of summer, temperatures were usually at least fifteen degrees cooler along the lake than they were in Cloquet. The jetty was also a good place to watch the giant iron ore carriers pass back and forth under the Aerial Lift Bridge. Those huge ships, to us, were dream material. To someday work the big vessels and travel the inland seas was something of a universal ambition among boys our age, and a few from Cloquet eventually did. In a sense we were kindred souls with the Tom Sawyers and Huck Finns on the lower Mississippi who dreamed of growing up to become river boat pilots in Mark Twain's time.

(Of the three of us, Bob Barr was the only one who actually shipped on a lake boat. He signed as a coalpasser on an ore carrier bound out of Duluth for Toledo, Ohio. His summation of the experience was, "I never knew there was so damn much coal in the whole world!" All three of us served in the navy during World War II, partly because, I suspect, of our boyhood attraction to the ore boats.)

Sometimes we bicycled the "old road" nine miles to Carlton and on to Jay Cooke State Park. The big attraction there was the swinging footbridge suspended over the boiling rapids and falls of the beer-colored waters of the St. Louis River. Constructed by either the Civilian Conservation Corps or the Works Project Administration, the bridge hung loosely from a pair of steel cables running between massive stone towers on either side of the maelstrom. Because of the length of the span and the sag on the cables, the structure was prone to considerable swing and belly-rising bounces. Riding bicycles across it was risky if not foolhardy. The bounce and sway had the potential to catapult the unwary to a rock-slamming, drowning death in the river. We did it anyway, adrenalin soaring marvelously as we defied the gods. (A bunch of years later, I took my own children to Jay Cook State Park. I had told them about the wonderful swinging bridge, its thrills and chills that had spiced my boyhood. Alas, the adult world of playground regulators had been there, no doubt flanked by a pot full of lawyers with briefs stuffed to overflowing with liability clauses. The bridge was a solid unit. A bulldozer couldn't move it. Oh sure, it's safer, but . . . isn't there a point where life can become too risk free?)

One fall day as we were wheeling around Jay Cooke Park, a boy and a girl on a picnic outing started a fire in the woods near the river to roast marshmallows. A sudden, gale-force wind came up without warning. The fire, mostly fueled by tinder-dry leaves (there had been no rain for weeks) was scattered quickly into the parched forest. The only thing that saved the park and possibly the whole of northern Minnesota was the close proximity of a C.C.C. camp geared for such emergencies. I did not know either the boy or the girl at the time, but a dozen years later and two thousand miles to the west, I married that girl.

The two Bobs and I never gave the dangers of hitchhiking a thought. Sometimes, out of sheer boredom, we'd thumb our way the nine miles to Carlton and back just to be moving. Bob Sundeen and I had our first motorcycle ride on one of those trips. A man on an Indian bike (the Indian Motorcycle Company folded during the Great Depression) fitted with a sidecar picked us up in Scanlon, Minnesota, and hauled us the six miles to Carlton at speeds exceeding seventy-five miles per hour. Hanging on for dear life, squinting our eyes and gritting our teeth against masses of mosquitoes and black flies, we chalked up another thrill of the open road.

In our earliest teens we had become well aware of the existence of girls from a distance. We spent considerable time discussing and fantasying about them but weren't quite ready to move on to

higher levels of lust and carnal knowledge. We were prepared, however, if by some extraordinary stroke of luck, we should be cast into
a den of licentious nymphomaniacs (you'll note the plurality of the
noun; if we were going, we were going big). Most every teen-aged
boy I knew packed a set of three talismanic condoms (we called
them rubbers or, more wickedly, French safes) in his wallet.
Unused, they eventually yellowed and rotted away, leaving telltale
rings pressed permanently into the leather. We purchased the condoms at the gasoline station on the corner of Eleventh Street and
Cloquet Avenue. Depending on who was on duty, small, porno-
graphic comic books featuring Dick Tracy, Tess True heart, Tillie
the Toiler and what they did when they weren't in the Sunday paper
were sometimes available.

Bobby Barr and I had our first slight brush with an "older
woman" on one of our hitchhiking trips to Carlton. We were on
our way back to Cloquet when a lovely, red-haired lady driving a
shiny, new green Plymouth sedan pulled to the side of the road in
answer to our raised thumbs. Running to the car which had been
moving at a good clip and stopped about thirty yards ahead of us,
Bob easily outdistanced me (he was fast and could outsprint most
boys his age). He opened the front passenger's door and started to
get in. Suddenly, his whole body stiffened. He let go of the door
handle as if it was burning his fingers. Quickly opening the back
door, he climbed in. I was amazed that he'd abandoned the favored
front seat, but as soon as I had one foot inside the car, I understood
his generosity. The woman's skirt, green to match her auto and
accentuate her marcelled hair, was up around her waist. Long, black
garter straps stretched to the tops of diaphanous silk hose gift wrap-
ping a pair of very shapely legs.

I don't know if the lady had panties on or not. I do know that
she never made any effort to pull down her skirt. Sadly, in retrospect,
I spent the six miles to Scanlon where she let us off, sweating and res-
olutely staring at my own feet.

Fifteen was a magic age for teen-agers. We were suddenly
deemed by the state to be old enough to operate automobiles on
Minnesota's highways. Reaching that coveted birthday, we hurried to
the courthouse in Carlton where, without any test, eye exam, or
demonstration of driving skills, we laid down fifty cents on the
counter and received our drivers' licenses. After that, our horizons
were only limited by our abilities to wheedle our parents for the use
of the family cars and the price of gasoline.

(Just recently, my wife and I visited her sister in Minneapolis. My sister-in-law was showing us the city, driving us around as hosts are prone to do, not considering you've just driven two thousand miles and momentarily detest automobiles. I noted that she spent a lot of time searching for parking places she could pull into straight. The few times she backed into spaces, we needed a sack lunch to sustain us between car and curb. I jokingly asked her how she ever managed to acquire a driver's license. "The same way you did!" she retorted. "Went to Carlton, paid fifty cents, and have made sure it never lapses so I won't have to take the test.")

My father and Martin Barr, Bob's dad, were assigned to new construction at the paper mill. They were erecting high steel and making a few extra dollars for the hazards involved. Naturally, the two of us were mesmerized by the thought of our fathers walking the I-beams at great heights, manning rivet guns to put together the framework of a tall building. With a need to imitate them, we turned our attention to Cloquet's water tower.

The tower, a riveted steel tank sitting on four sturdy legs of the same material, was probably erected on top of its hill on the west side of town shortly after the Great Fire of 1918. It was, and may still be, the tallest structure in Cloquet.

Messing around on the water tower had to be a clandestine, nighttime operation. Getting caught would have meant, at the least, a very uncomfortable discussion with Chief of Police Reed and hell to pay at home. At first, we were content to squeeze between the bars of the padlocked barrier guarding the base of the ladder that ran up one leg of the structure and climb to the catwalk. The catwalk circled around the bottom part of the tank, and from there we could see all of Cloquet, its many lights giving our small community the semblance of a big city. It was inevitable, of course, that by our third nightly ascent of the tower, we were leaving the catwalk and continuing on a second ladder up to the edge of the tank's inverted cone-shaped roof. From there, we'd scuttle crab-like up the sloping surface to tag the round ball at the highest point. Then came the idea to walk the horizontal girders tying the tower's legs together.

There were three sets of girders; those on the lowest level were about thirty feet off the ground, the middle set an equal distance above the first, and the top ones placed a final thirty feet below the tank. Looking down from ninety feet, the distance seemed a mile. Adding to the illusion of great height was the fact that the structure sat on top of a steep hill.

Bob and I decided that if our fathers could work on high steel, we could certainly walk around at least one of the levels of leg-tying girders on the water tower. Of course, being thirteen or fourteen years old, we went for the highest set.

Our chosen girders were six to eight inches wide, but ninety feet up in the night sky, they resembled finished two-by-fours turned on edge. Bob squeezed through the strap-iron cage enclosing the ladder, stood poised on the girder for a long minute and ever so slowly began inching his way along the steel ribbon until he reached the next leg. Easing his body around the upright, he paused and called, "Come on! You can do it."

My knees suddenly went weak. I slipped through the protective cage and stood trembling on the girder, both hands frozen onto the tower leg. Up until that moment, I'd never experienced any fear of heights; but, looking at that thread of steel I was supposed to walk, all I could see was my soon-to-be-smashed body cartwheeling through space.

I wanted to do it. I didn't want Bob to be one up on me. But, I couldn't.

"I can't," I admitted shamefully. "It's too dangerous."

Bob said nothing. He continued slowly working his way from leg to leg until he'd boxed the tower and returned to the ladder. To his credit and my everlasting gratitude, he never ragged or belittled me, and I don't think he ever told another soul.

I never climbed the water tower again.

24

Junior and Senior High School

After all these years, the eighth, ninth, and tenth grades at Cloquet High School more or less run together in my memory. I remember the period mostly as a good time in my life. Academic subjects posed no problems. Also, compulsory music and art classes terminated at the end of the seventh grade to my everlasting relief and, no doubt, that of the teachers whose classroom thresholds I would never again be forced to cross. I never could sing and from kindergarten on had trouble keeping my crayon smears inside the lines.

Although I thought I hated him at the time, my eighth grade math instructor, Mr. Walter Nosek, was undoubtedly the best teacher I ever had. He was a very strict no-nonsense disciplinarian. There wasn't a student who didn't live in mortal fear of the man. Incomplete homework was unthinkable, and we hardly knew who sat behind us in his class because we didn't dare turn around to find out. I learned more math in the eighth grade than ever before or since.

Quite the opposite situation prevailed immediately across the hall from Mr. Nosek's room. My class schedule took me from math to social studies, from complete autocratic control to pandemonium and total anarchy. The lady who taught the subject had lost command of her students at least twenty years earlier, and we, I'm sorry to say, made her life a living hell. Why the administration didn't step in and apply the rubber hose (a very effective order restorer, it wasn't used very often) to a few of us or reassign the woman to an elementary school, I'll never understand. The constant noise level and the bowl-style light fixtures heaped to overflowing with spitballs must have told them something. A simple note to our fathers would have made angels out of most of us, but nothing of the sort was ever done. Then, as if the teacher didn't have enough problems, came the advent of the ten-shot squirt gun. The lady would turn her back to write on the chalkboard and streams of water would slash across the room, rivulets fingering down the slates on either side of her.

A girl with a monumental, awe-inspiring bosom wangled the seat directly behind mine in the social studies class. Her name was Bonnie, and she had a big, syrupy crush on me, which, unfortunately, I was too stupid to appreciate. Her unabashed adoration, which she publicized with chalked graffiti of hearts and plus signs on walls, sidewalks, and other highly visible places, caused me considerable embarrassment among my friends. I looked to the water pistol for revenge. Arms folded across my chest, fully primed ten-shot tucked under my left armpit, I kept the girl constantly under the gun, so to speak. Feigning interest in the teacher's soporific lectures concerning the Angles, the Saxons, the Gauls, and a couple of varieties of Goths, I'd position myself with the weapon pointed directly at Bonnie's nose. At the sight of the brass-colored muzzle, she'd squeal under her breath and squirm as if I were attempting things on her body other than fire control. With ten shots at my disposal, I'd stretch the water torture over an entire fifty-minute class period.

One day the teacher noticed the girl's constant movement to dodge the threatened spray and came over to her desk. "Do you feel all right, Bonnie?" she asked with obvious concern. Taking a closer look, she exclaimed, "Why, dear, you're just dripping with perspiration! Would you like to go to the nurse's office?" Bonnie declined, insisting that she was fine. She didn't give me away, although she looked as if she'd just stepped out of a shower.

The squirt gun craze mushroomed wildly. We reached a point where ten shots didn't carry us through a normal class period, and almost every boy tucked a jar of water into his desk for emergencies. Of course, the inevitable happened. Bob Sundeen, not cut out to lead a successful life of crime, accidentally dumped his full jar into his lap.

Under normal conditions in that classroom, the incident would have probably gone unnoticed in the general hubbub, but it was our last period of the week, and we were deep in the midst of a written test, a difficult situation when one has spent most of his time playing Wyatt Earp at the O.K. Corral and not read the textbook or listened to the lectures. The room was silent except for an occasional anguished sigh from some soul who'd come to the realization that he might be forced to repeat social studies again the next year when Bob gasped, "Ar-rr-rgh! Jeez!" as water cascaded into his lap and onto the floor.

Miss Social Studies was on him in a flash. Every nerve taut, fingernails biting into her palms, she exploded, "What are you doing with water in your desk?"

There was no denying the evidence. We all waited expectantly for the inescapable confession. Bob looked hopefully about for help. There was none. He had to say something. His answer came in the form of a barely audible question. "I get thirsty?" The class roared while Miss Social Studies fled the room in tears just as the bell signaled the end of the week. We were all retested on the following Monday. As far as I know, the water incident was never mentioned again.

Most of my peers looked forward to attending shop classes in the eighth grade. I did, too, until I tackled the first project, squaring a board with a handsaw and plane. I never mastered it. When I squared one end, I unsquared the other. I turned piles of lumber into shavings and sawdust to no avail. To this day, I detest working with hand tools.

I wasn't alone. Bob Barr was a shade better at carpentry than I, but not much (he eventually became a very successful funeral director). Jack Campbell, a future U.S. Army colonel, did about as well as Bob Barr. Everybody, it seemed, was more adept than I with the possible exception of a feisty kid by the name of Duane "Duke" Arntson. Duke's and my shop abilities were about even. We were still attempting to square boards long after others were carrying home fine tables, china cabinets, and the like.

I did, eventually, finish a shoeshine box complete with a lid and footrest. No, it wasn't precisely square, and the cover soon fell off, but if the teacher, Mr. Cyril Gardiner, is still among the living, I want him to know that it has been in use for more than fifty years and is holding up well—without the lid, of course.

Eighth grade algebra was a snap. Mr. Nosek's expert tutelage had a lot to do with it, I'm sure. Near the end of the academic year, however, we had a short introduction to the mysteries of geometry, and I found myself floundering. With school winding down for the summer, I chalked up my confusion to spring fever and gave it no more thought until, suddenly, vacation was over and Miss Selma Larson was covering her blackboards with mind-numbing obtuse and acute angles and other equally incomprehensible matter.

I gave the subject my best shot, but by the end of the third week, Miss Larson was approaching page thirty in the text while I was still trying to decipher page one. Like an Arab folding his tent and moving to the city, I closed the book and told myself, "To hell with it!"

Although it was a waste, I did attend class regularly. Sometimes as I sat there in an uncomprehending daze, Miss Larson would turn from her incessant scribbling on the board, look into my glazed eyes, and say, "Jerry Carlson, you're not getting this!" She was right. My test scores were irrefutable evidence to the fact.

Roy Fay had the seat directly behind me in Miss Larson's class, and he spoke geometry fluently. Once, for something to do, I copied Roy's homework assignment in the most minute detail and turned it in as my own. When the papers were returned, Roy had a score in the upper nineties while mine indicated severe congenital moronity. I asked Miss Larson, "How can this be? Roy's and my papers are identical except for the names at the top."

"That's why," was her answer. I didn't argue.

Report card grades in the Cloquet schools were given in percentages, seventy-five percent being the lowest possible passing score. Long before the final mark in geometry was posted on my card, I knew I had failed and Miss Larson knew I had failed. But, when I slowly opened the dreaded missive, like a poker player who has drawn to an inside straight checking his cards, there was a final grade of seventy-five. It must have been a frustrating year for her, too, and neither of us had any desire to repeat it. Miss Larson and I had, at long last, found common ground.

25

Puppy Love

During the summer between my fourteenth and fifteenth birthdays, I fell hopelessly in love for the first time. The torment is commonly known as puppy love. If it is truly canine in origin, it certainly explains why old dogs sometimes whimper and twitch in their sleep.

The girl lived with her family about two blocks from our shack on Carlton Avenue. We were members of the same class in school, attended the same church and were totally oblivious of one another for years. Suddenly, maybe because I had repeated the second grade, our physical development coincided, our hormones went crazy at the same time, and we were in love. God, she was beautiful!

Bob Sundeen and I had just begun seriously looking over the available girls, riding our bicycles to the far reaches of the community in rooster-like quests without much success. Then, on a pleasant summer's evening as we sat on the curb across the street from my house, wondering which compass heading to wheel on next, she pedaled out of nowhere on her blue and white bike, smiled and said, "Hi." She hadn't gone fifty yards (she wasn't moving very fast) before we had her flanked on both sides like a pair of destroyers escorting a sleek cruiser.

As a fiery red sun slipped behind the western horizon, the three of us stood around in her front yard talking the normal prattle of fourteen-year-olds, Bob and I trying to impress her and she pretending to be impressed. I don't remember the preliminaries if there were any, but suddenly, without warning, she bussed me squarely on the lips and skipped off into her house.

Bob reacted with his favorite exclamation, "Jeez!" I walked on turbulent air for the next year.

Our love affair sizzled from day one. We couldn't and didn't want to keep our hands off each other, but we always stopped short of going over the cliff. We were trapped in a confusing Victorian time warp. It was the period in history when Rhett Butler was just contemplating uttering the word "damn" in front of Scarlett O'Hara and shocked movie goers. It was a time when true love meant you waited until marriage, a time of agonizing, exquisite suffering.

Finding a place to peck and pet wasn't always easy. We weren't old enough to use the family car, and the necessary privacy was not available in either of our homes. We finally found a quiet, dark, secluded haven at the south entrance of Garfield School. One of the few buildings in Cloquet to survive the Great Fire of 1918, the old bricks must have been tempered by the conflagration, because we certainly generated enough heat to take out lesser constructions. A summer's evening behind Garfield School followed by another round at the girl's door after escorting her home, and I could scarcely walk! The word among my peers was that straining against impossible weight would bring relief. I still have muscles developed in my struggles to pick up parked cars on my way home.

Winters in northern Minnesota cause all sorts of hardships, not the least of which is the crimp they can throw into the path of young love. It's simply too cold. Romance is difficult to nurture when the participants are buried under layers of heavy woolen clothing and hobbled with bulky mittens. But, we persevered.

The public library was warm and afforded moments of occasional privacy behind the shelves. Luther League meetings in the church basement were made tolerable with a stolen kiss in the kitchen while breaking out the cookies and Kool-Aid. The community Civic Center sponsored Dri-Nite dances that gave young lovers a chance to get close. Where there's a will, there's a way.

Our passion lasted through the winter. But sometime, in our second summer, we split. I don't remember why anymore. Maybe we reached the end of the road, the place where the ride would have become more than we dared to handle at fifteen. We dated once a couple years later. I'd returned to Cloquet from the West Coast for a short visit. She was going steady with another boy but agreed to go out with me for old times sake. I made an awkward, stupid, uncalled for, adolescent pass. She slapped me good. I had it coming.

I don't know what life eventually dealt the girl. I am glad that she was my first love.

26

Culture and Distractions

Cloquet didn't offer much in the way of cultural diversions; the annual junior and senior high school plays were as close as we came to "theater," and art was a Varga or Petty girl calendar on a gasoline station wall. Music was reasonably taken care of by the Cloquet City Band, a group of local musicians under the direction of Mr. L.D. Gerin who gave weekly evening concerts throughout the summer in Pinehurst Park. However, during the 1930s when hustlers were hard put to turn a dime, some imaginative entrepreneurs appeared from time to time to add "outside" sources of spice and knowledge to our lives.

I saw my first whale in Cloquet, Minnesota, far from the sea. A flimflam man brought one into town in a railroad car. It was a small baleen whale that had washed up on a coastal beach somewhere. We paid ten cents to see it because it was bigger than any St. Louis River catfish we'd ever heard of. In the heat of summer, we could still smell it for some time after it had gone.

Another huckster gathered our dimes by bringing in a live anaconda on the train, a long, scary, green monster with a black head the size of a gunny sack full of potatoes. It laid in a trough of water and had a huge bulge in its midsection, a pig it would spend weeks digesting.

Then there was Bonnie Parker's and Clyde Barrow's last automobile, the Ford in which they were shot to death on a Louisiana road by a posse under the command of a Texas ranger. If I remember correctly, this was a freebie compliments of a local car dealer. The auto was a sieve of bullet holes, and the man accompanying the display took great pains to point out dried bloodstains and bits of brain splattered about the vehicle's interior.

Carnivals were summertime diversions most of the community anticipated. Two or three a season would roll into town, pitch their tents and booths, and set up their rides in White's field on the

Old Carlton Road. It took the operators about three nights to clean out Cloquet's loose change before they moved on. As boys, of course, we practically lived on the midway for the complete run, spending our meager resources mostly on rides. Adults were more interested in the games (bingo, baseball throws, shooting galleries, and the like) and taking in the sideshows.

The fight tent was always popular with most everybody. To attract attention, the barker would rake an iron pipe over the rivets on a section of an old hot water tank. As soon as a crowd had assembled, three or four pugilist-types in tights (usually faded red-flannel long johns) would strut onto the outside stage, flexing their biceps and challenging all-comers. A couple of local men, the Olson brothers, usually volunteered to defend the honor of Cloquet, having been contracted by the carnival's advance men long before the shows hit town. The matches consisted mainly of professional-style wrestling entertainment, but most of us believed it was for real. That is, we believed until one group, not willing to meet the Olson brothers' terms, tried to foist one of their own men off as a Cloquet native. Bouncing onto the stage to answer the challenge, he was asked where he was from. "Cloquet," he answered, pronouncing it Klo-Kwet and losing all credibility in that one utterance.

Another big attraction was the girlie show, a joy to the men and a chance for the ladies to act properly shocked. Every carnival had its Little Eve or Little Egypt, but the one who stands out in my memory is the Bomber. Platinum blonde, brassy, she whirled long tassels like propellers on the front of her twin engines. She could twirl them right or left or two different directions at once. She was the talk of the town.

The Tri-state Fair in Superior, Wisconsin, was an annual must for our family. We usually took the road through Oliver, Wisconsin, to get there. The route was almost a carnival ride in itself. A very narrow two-lane highway to begin with, it had the unique distinction of being paved on only one side from the bridge in Oliver all the way to Superior, a distance of ten or so miles over Wisconsin's rolling terrain. Of course, everyone drove on the paved portion regardless of which direction they were going, leading to some head-on collisions and countless hairbreadth misses.

One of my first trips to the fair taught me great respect for electricity. I must have been six or seven years old at the time. Hawkers on the midway were pushing multicolored canes with tweeter birds attached on short strings. I pestered my folks until I got one.

Our kitchen on Tenth Street was lighted at the time by a single bulb suspended from the ceiling. The light was screwed into a double socket, one side of which was empty. My tweeter bird cane had a metal tip. Immediately after arriving home from the fair, I probed it into the open socket. Instant lightning! A blinding, blue flash, a shower of sparks, a "what the hell!" from my father, and the house plunged into darkness. The wooden shaft of the cane protected me from electrocution, but its metal tip was burned away along with a melt-down of the light receptacle.

Every summer brought at least one air show to the Cloquet Airport, a mowed hayfield west of town marked with a ragged, faded wind sock. My father, enamored with aircraft of all kinds, made sure we attended. The shows were all basically the same: some stunt flying, a wing walker, and sometimes a parachute jump to attract a crowd for the purpose of selling airplane rides.

My folks, having learned very early that tending to and amusing two kids was a lot easier than trying to keep one happy, almost always had me bring along a friend on our excursions. As a result, Bob Sundeen and I had our first plane ride together in an open-cockpit, fabric-covered Waco biplane, five minutes of thrills in the sky for five dollars. The pilot made a few quick, steep banking turns over Cloquet while Bob and I hung on to a handlebar in the front cockpit and squinted against the wind. The effect was much like our first motorcycle ride except that we were well above the ceiling of mosquitoes and black flies.

Why my father didn't take up flying, I've never understood. He loved it. His first ride in an airplane ended in a forced, dead-stick landing that convinced his pilot to give up flying but didn't faze Dad. The pilot was a friend of Dad's in Crosby, Minnesota, named Paul Henning. Henning bought a Jenny biplane just after World War I, and it wasn't long before he and my father came up with the bright idea to hunt ducks in their own medium—up in the sky. I suspect there was a little preflight firewater consumption involved in preparation for the event, but be that as it may, Dad positioned himself in the rear cockpit while the pilot operated from the front. They'd buzz a lake to bring up the birds, circle, and come back like the Red Baron with shotgun blazing. It was great sport until the radiator on the water-cooled machine began to boil and the engine sputtered, coughed, and died. Paul Henning brought them down in a cornfield. Fences snapped, a large swath of the crop was destroyed, and a farmer was very angry. Mr. Henning sold the plane, thanked God he was still alive, and went to work for the post office.

Many years later, my wife and I were living in White Mountain, Alaska, when my folks came for a visit. We made arrangements for a bush pilot friend to pick them up in Fairbanks. The pilot, Bill Peterson, had been logging hours around the clock, taking advantage of the long summer days. He put his Beechcraft Bonanza into the air, gave Dad a couple rudimentary lessons and a compass heading and dropped off to sleep with, "Fly it, Frank. Anything comes up, wake me."

Dad flew the ship, with a little tight-lipped help from Mom in the backseat, across western Alaska to the Bering Sea. He never forgot it. Before his death at age seventy-six, most of his memory gone to the ravages of hardening of the arteries, he never ceased telling of the time he flew a plane in Alaska.

The Dri-Nite dances at the Civic Center were designed to keep young people wholesomely occupied and out of mischief. They didn't always succeed.

Some older teen-agers began using the dances to experiment with alcohol, mostly drinking themselves sick and upchucking into the snowdrifts behind the building. Of course, some of my friends and I wanted to be part of the action. Our problem was where to get the booze.

Bob Sundeen, Jack Purcell, and I were mulling over our situation one Dri-Nite when it occurred to me that our church's congregation had celebrated Holy Communion the Sunday before and that there must have been some wine left over. We headed for the church.

The building was dark as we slipped in through the unlocked front door. Moving furtively up the center aisle, we entered the vestry to the right of the altar. Closing the door to the small office behind us, we switched on the light. Opening desk drawers, checking behind books lining shelves protected by glass doors, we were about to give up when I finally found the bottle tucked behind some boxes in a floor-level cupboard. Encased in a gray velvet sack with a drawstring closer, it was about two-thirds full.

As I pulled the wine bottle from its bag, Jack Purcell whispered, "We shouldn't be doing this."

Bob Sundeen, a tremor in his voice, squeaked, "Jeez! We're stealing the blood of Christ!"

"If it is," I observed nervously, "it's got a government tax stamp!"

We passed the bottle around for a couple of hefty swallows apiece, put the nearly empty container back into its velvet sack, and returned it to the cupboard. Turning off the light, we exited the building as quietly as we came.

Whether the wine was ever missed, we never heard. Many years later, however, Bob Sundeen admitted to no small number of sleepless nights following the incident as his conscience goaded him, and he contemplated eternity in hell. The experience must have also dissuaded him from any further thoughts of criminal activity. He was eventually elected Carlton County Treasurer, retiring after many years with perfectly balanced ledgers.

My mother never gave up her struggle to make a Lutheran out of me. It was a hopeless, thankless endeavor. I considered Sunday school an infringement on my time and church services a deathly bore. Then came two years of confirmation classes—on Saturdays yet! This on top of delivering those weekly bulletins.

Confirmation classes meant memorizing the catechism—no questions, no comments, no weighing of alternatives, just memorize, repeat, believe or face damnation. Parrots, I decided early on, would make good Christians. To this day, I have trouble with angels; how can supposedly rational human beings believe in the existence of humanoid creatures with wings and yet deny with certainty the possibility of Santa Claus and the Easter Bunny?

Only once, for a fleeting moment, did I consider reconsidering my nonbelief of an all-controlling supreme being. It was about a year after I nearly rolled our car.

Turning fifteen, I picked up my driver's license in Carlton and started pestering my folks to teach me to drive. A man of little patience, the grinding of gears and jumping-jack starts tended to unnerve my father, so my mother took on the job. Mom soon had my basic moves smoothed out, and the game of finding excuses to use the car began.

Over the years, Mom had suffered a series of miscarriages and related "female problems" and was recuperating at home from one of these episodes when I came close to flipping our wheels. The old 1932 Chevy had been traded in on a used 1936 Chevrolet coupe when, willing to do anything short of cold-blooded murder to get behind the steering wheel, I volunteered to attend a Sunday church service without being dragged if I could take the car. Permission granted, I headed toward the church, picking up Bob Sundeen and his brother Elwood along the way. We arrived at our destination, passed it, and kept on going.

Joy-riding through the countryside west of town, we came over the crest of a steep hill and were hurtling down the other side at about sixty-five miles per hour when it registered on me that the very bottom of the slope was a mass of foot-deep ruts in loose gravel. I hit the brakes. The car began to fish-tail on the road's pebbly surface. I knew if we took those ruts sideways, we were in big trouble. Releasing the brakes, I grasped the wheel in a death grip and hung on as we plowed into the mess. For a split second we were all over the road, then came a couple of hard bumps and spine-jamming jolts, and we were stopped, still upright but back-end-to in the ditch.

Climbing out, we couldn't see any damage to the vehicle. I restarted the engine, the Sundeen boys pushed, and we were back on the road.

Moving considerably slower, we returned to Cloquet. Cruising up Cloquet Avenue, we were waved over to the curb by one of the Vnuk brothers who also attended Cloquet schools. He informed us that there was "something wrong" with the Chevy's right rear wheel. Letting one of the Sundeen boys drive, I watched as the car moved a few feet up the street. My guts turned to jelly. Vnuk was right. The wheel looked like it was about to fall off. My father was going to kill me. Worse, I'd never be allowed to drive again.

That wheel had to be fixed before Dad found out about it. I drove the Chevrolet several more blocks and pulled into Angell's Tire and Battery Shop.

Bill Angell, the proprietor, always took Sunday off, turning the business over to one of his two high school-age sons to man the gasoline pumps. His youngest boy, Honey, a good friend of mine, had drawn the duty this particular day. Honey looked the situation over and decided the problem was not a loose wheel but a bent one. He couldn't fix it. He suggested removing the wheel and putting on the spare. This entailed a little more than just a straight exchange. The spare was a worn tire; the one on the bent wheel was fairly new. It took us a while, but the double switch was accomplished.

Now I had a monkey on my back. I knew the spare wheel was bent, but my father didn't. How was I ever going to get it straightened without him knowing? I lived in dread that one or the other of my folks might have a flat tire and bring my crime to light. I sweat it through that summer (1941), the following winter, and into spring again. I even tried praying a couple of times. It was not a question of would I be found out, but when.

It was another sunny, spring Sunday. I was sitting in church with my mother and getting absolutely no solace from the droning noises emanating from the pulpit, thinking, no, worrying about that accursed wheel and wondering if, like Job, rending my clothes and dumping ashes on my head would help. I had about decided that Job was another of those Biblical masochists who liked to make themselves miserable, when there was a resounding crash of automobiles beyond the yellow-orange translucent glass of the church's windows.

I, of little faith, began to hope. I'd parked our car on the corner. Somehow, I just knew it had been hit. The preacher, a man set on a course, ground on like a molasses-driven millstone. I chafed. I squirmed. I waited. The choir marched out. The minister marched out. The big sinners from the front pews marched out. Our turn finally came. I bounded, nay, flew down the cement steps leading from the church and ran to our car. It was beautiful. The rear-mounted spare, encased in its metal cover, was rammed into the trunk. I was saved by a hit-and-run driver.

Thirty years later, pestered by a pair of teen-agers of my own who were itching to drive, I mentioned the incident with the long-gone Chevy in my father's presence. To my amazement, he became really peeved. The fact that I'd had an accident didn't upset him. It was the thought that I'd gotten away with it.

Reaching driving age gave us a lot of new mobility and pushed back the boundaries of our world. It also nearly killed three of us.

Jack Campbell, Bob Barr, and I had driven twenty or so miles to the Pike Lake Roller Skating Rink. We were on our way back to Cloquet about eleven P.M. There was a nip of fall in the air, a bright, cold moon silhouetting the dark trees along the roadside. The windows of Jack's 1930 Chevrolet coupe were rolled up against the chill.

We were talking and joshing each other about the various girls we'd met at the rink when Bob asked, "What's that bright light over there?"

Jack and I looked to the east. Jack answered, "The moon."

"Can't be," Bob disagreed. "The moon's over there." He pointed to the southeast.

"Could be a light at the Duluth airport," I guessed.

We continued moving southward toward the Nopeming Junction where the Pike Lake Road intersected the main trunk highway between Duluth and the Twin Cities. The strange light began to bother us. It seemed to be moving in our direction from the east at a rapid rate, but, although we weren't too familiar with the area, we were fairly certain there were no major roads in that direction. We had just entered a long, gradual curve in the highway when, suddenly, the light was on us. We heard a train's whistle and felt the tracks under us at the same instant. Because of the curve, we had to move along the rails diagonally for some distance before we could clear them.

Jack didn't speed up, nor did he slow down. We bounced off the last track just as an ore-jammer ripped past behind us, whistle screaming. We cleared the train by less than three feet.

We continued on a couple of miles to the Nopeming Junction, stopped and got out of the car. It was then that our knees began to shake.

27

Endings

December 7, 1941, eighteen days short of my sixteenth birthday, the Japanese bombed Pearl Harbor. I'd never heard of the place.

My mother was in Raiters' Hospital recovering from surgery, and Dad and I were baching. As was usual on Sundays, my father was at the paper mill doing maintenance and repair work. In Mom's absence, he did all the cooking, and I was his delegated scullery help. I was up to my elbows in dirty dishes when news of the attack came over the radio. Later that afternoon, I visited my mother and told her I'd heard that the Japanese had bombed Hawaii. She seemed pensive and said softly, "I know. . . . It means war."

The next day at school the talk was all Pearl Harbor. The Japanese were crazy. A little country like that—we'd put them away in six months or less. Some of us wondered about Gordy Caza. He'd quit school the year before and had just recently joined the army. He'd been stationed in Hawaii only a short time before the Japanese attack.

The initial excitement died out in a few days. The draft boards had been in operation for some time; my uncles Willie and Oscar, among others, had been called up early. Gas rationing and a national thirty-five miles-per-hour speed limit were instituted almost immediately, and people began taking part in scrap drives. Otherwise, the war had little effect on my age group, and life went on much as usual. I went on the annual Luther League sleigh ride. (Bob Sundeen and I were sparking the same girl, but she was true to another. I did, however, take great satisfaction in tossing Reverend Rossing off the moving sleigh during the rough-and-tumble of a king of the hill skirmish.) Then, of course, belonging to a Norwegian church, there was the Christmas lutefisk-and-meatball supper complete with lingonberries, which neither war nor pestilence could ever stop. (Mrs. Art Ogren and others of the Ladies' Aid would soak the dried codfish in lye water in the church basement for weeks preceding the event. They never had to advertise; the assault on Cloquet's collective olfactory nerves said it all.) Most of the community attended the lutefisk fest. The French Catholics from a section of Cloquet known as Little Canada were the champion consumers. Ice skating, school, and Dri-Nite dances continued through the winter as always. At winter's end, May 1942, I finished my sophomore year unaware it was to be my last year of high school.

Early in July, my folks dropped a bomb of their own—they asked if I'd mind leaving Cloquet. Dad was fed up with his job at the paper company. The new construction phase at the plant had come to an end, and his wages were cut back to mill scale (seventy-five cents an hour). The extra money for working construction had finally paid off the old Depression Era grocery bill and most of my and Mom's accrued medical expenses. At age forty-two, I suspect Dad felt it was now or never if he was going to make a change.

My immediate reaction to their proposal was one of ambivalence. I really didn't want to leave my friends or change schools, but I also didn't have any overwhelmingly strong ties or loyalties to the community. School had become a predictable drag. During my sophomore year, I managed to schedule two consecutive study halls the last periods of the day; I'd do my homework assignments during the first one and skip the second. I'd discovered that if you didn't sign the class enrollment sheet the first day, no one ever expected you to be there. I certainly wasn't looking forward to two more years of the same. Also, we still lived in Gunnard Johnson's shack, and I was still making up the studio couch each night for bed.

The folks didn't pressure me one way or the other. Dad considered education important and was prepared to hang tough in Cloquet if I felt strongly about finishing school there. I slept on the proposition one night. The next morning I said, "Let's go."

On August 12, 1942, our total worldly possessions packed into the trunk of the 1936 Chevrolet coupe, Mom, Dad, Schultz, and I headed west, our tentative destination: Portland, Oregon. Our last stop in Cloquet was a brief one at the cemetery; Mom wanted a final good-bye at my brother Richard's grave. Somehow, she must have sensed she'd never see it again. Thirty-four years later, with the generous and compassionate assistance of the founders of the Barr Brothers' Funeral Home, I placed her ashes in that same grave.

Epilogue

The many years since my departure from Cloquet, Minnesota, have been filled with ships, high arctic adventure, schools attended and taught, mountains climbed, and rivers run—all bringing their diverse varieties of people into my life. Without people, the good, the bad, the indifferent, the world is just physical geography. We, as human beings, are to a great extent the sum of those who touch our lives. For better or for worse, the pages of this book have introduced you to some who contributed to my formative years and, possibly, in some small way, I to theirs.